The Rise of Data in Educ
collection, visualisation and uses

Comparative Histories of Education

Series Editors: MARTIN LAWN & ANTÓNIO NÓVOA

Created as part of national narratives of progress, and bounded by state borders and systems, histories of education now require an expansion into the horizontal plane, to develop an intellectual field focusing upon objects, ideas and relations, across borders and sites.

This series is intended to encourage the exploration of new questions and areas, through which comparative histories of education can be formed, recognising heterogeneity, flows of ideas and technologies, cross-border designs, international networks and material collections. It also aims to encourage contributions from different disciplines, raise historical and comparative arguments for the study of educational issues, and encourage creative approaches that can contribute to a renewal of educational historiography.

Previous volumes in the series

Modelling the Future
exhibitions and the materiality of education
Edited by MARTIN LAWN, 2009
ISBN 978-1-873927-27-4

An Atlantic Crossing?
the work of the International Examinations
Inquiry, its researchers, methods and influence
Edited by MARTIN LAWN, 2008
ISBN 978-1-873927-26-7

Materialities of Schooling
design, technology, objects, routines
Edited by MARTIN LAWN & IAN GROSVENOR, 2005
ISBN 978-10873927-30-4

The Rise of Data in Education Systems:
collection, visualisation and uses

Edited by
MARTIN LAWN

Comparative Histories of Education
Series Editors: Martin Lawn & António Nóvoa

SYMPOSIUM
BOOKS

Symposium Books Ltd
PO Box 204 Didcot Oxford OX11 9ZQ United Kingdom
www.symposium-books.co.uk

Published in the United Kingdom, 2013

ISBN 978-1-873927-32-8

© Symposium Books, 2013

Printed and bound in the United Kingdom by Hobbs the Printers, Southampton
www.hobbs.uk.com

Contents

Introduction:
the rise of data in education

MARTIN LAWN

The use of data in education systems and the procedures by which they are constructed has not been a major part of the study of education, nor the histories of education systems. The foundation of education systems has utilised unevenly administrative records, pupil testing data, efficiency surveys, international projects and technological capacities, and the study of these system foundations has been sporadic. The engine of numerical data provision has been statistics, and especially its close connections to intelligence testing and factorial analyses. This has been a very influential movement but, at its heart, an extremely specialist one. Numerical data has a power of explanation in the governance of education because it is based upon an esoteric and unknowable set of techniques for many in the field. Also, it operates by excluding the values, ideas and politics that interest many students of education.

This collection of historical essays about the recording, collection and use of education data has its origin in the new sociology of statistics (Porter, 1996; Desrosières, 2002), which has opened out the history of statistics and shown the ways that it has developed conditionally, locally and culturally, and in close interaction with state construction. Science, the state and systems of education have been bound together. Making things countable is not purely a question of mathematics but of social purpose and of convention. When elites become weak, when politics is divided, and when system trust is low, then counting and comparison offer a way through the governing of systems, including education. Today, when the future can no longer be organised through meaningful projects by government, numerical data becomes a useful substitute for ideas.

The rise of data to describe, represent or explain education systems, and their constituent parts, is a mid-nineteenth-century invention, associated with the rise of schools and budgets, and also with the beginning of the Great Exhibitions or World's Fairs. Tabular data was used to record, often in only the broadest terms, an education system and its workings. This was most commonly administrative data, which was used in end-of-year budget tallies but not as the basis for analysis. Yet numerical data was not the only form of data used in education accounts. In the mid twentieth century, the data were likely to be visual images which the underlying captions treated as accurate representations of a system, sometimes when the narrative needed it or the tables were incomplete. The meaning of the visual data is produced alongside it and turns it into system information. Comparison, one of the key social science methodologies, soon began to be associated with the production of data, and in the late-nineteenth-century Exhibitions, comparison began to be associated with data and not just objects. Finding patterns within numerical data soon became a skill and a profession in itself, with statisticians as its keystone. At the national and later the international level, the late twentieth century saw the rise of the virtual system in which data occupies the physical place and the living person, allows them to be moved around, and to be viewed from different perspectives. To create the virtual world of data, and to make it stable and useful, whole silos of classifications and standards have to be agreed, and key terms, procedures, reliability and validity checks have to be produced continually.

Within the last few years, mainly quantitative data has gained enormous influence in education systems through the work of the Organisation for Economic Cooperation and Development (OECD), the European Commission and national system agencies. The creation and flow of data has become a powerful governing tool in education. But the development and growth of education data in contemporary modern education systems has been uneven, as national traditions and practices varied and statistical expertise was uncommon. Education data has moved out of local or national reports, collected by specialist and expert groups, and gradually into public representations of education, used widely by emerging or non-experts. Tests devised for one group became used with widely varying others, and results compared with other divergent groups. As international institutions began to collect their own data, or became repositories for evidence about cross-border flows, comparisons became easier. The visualisation of the data, and its range of techniques, has changed over time, especially in its movement from an expert to a public act. Data had to be explained to widening audience.

Numerical data has two potential capabilities, which have established its contemporary significance, especially in neoliberal states. It enables the redesign of the education system by measuring it. With its own capacity and contracts with commercial partners, the state in England has been able to create a new version of an education system while it still appears to have the same shape and features as in the past. Pupils, parents and teachers still tend to see the local authorities as being in place, with their own local schools, with recognisable teachers in 'normal' classrooms, and with the main stages of schooling recognisable since the 1950s. This physical state of education, viewed in bricks and objects and personnel, continues, and is still seen within visual data about the relations of its parts. Even when it appears distorted or dislocated with the sharp effects of local markets in education or the insertion of new school types, the schools and the system appears to continue seemingly unchanged.

The shift to governing through data in the United Kingdom has not only altered outside perceptions of schooling but it has also fundamentally altered the landscape and practices of education from within. Local and regional authorities are not the only players now. New software and new data companies have had enormous effects; they have created new conduits of information about schooling; they have enabled new digitised packets of data to flow around the system, following each pupil and their individual code identity; they have kept the system working for longer hours and have automated responses. While local areas had significant directors of education, the new managers of the virtual landscape of education are hidden elsewhere.

The capacity of the centre, the local and the school to produce a wide range of school data and to analyse it has increased beyond anything known earlier. A constant pressure to produce, analyse and act upon the data is now self-generating. New specialist skills and new managerial posts have been created at all levels. The local authority may continue to enact a 'governing' role through data interpretation and mediation with 'its' schools, in order to assist and support overwhelmed schools but some smaller authorities with fewer data skills may be more dependent on the centre and less able to offer independent strategic and contextual support. (Ozga et al, 2011).

As measurement and calculation have intensified, the state can 'see' more; its vision is wider and faster. The act of 'seeing', of making things governable, alters the observed (Lawn, 2011). This act of 'seeing' appears to be viral: system actors become believers, self-creating hubs of data production and flow, while other actors try to remain invisible and opaque in the system. It is not just a question of pressure or a new normativity in education. 'Seeing' has created a series of new mental, social and physical spaces (Lefebvre, 1991) across education, which in turn are interconnected with the wide range of governing surveillance activity in English society. This 'dystopic' turn in governing education in England and in different ways in Europe is dependent on deep twentieth-century roots. The technology of measurement has become a powerful international force; the tools of testing and the statistical techniques of factorial studies have been viral and not containable within borders or institutions (Smyth, 2008). It offers a way of decoding the pupil over time, and managing administration and policy in developing systems.

Data are shaped through their circulation from local production by national statistical agencies, through scientific congresses, to international exchange via supra-national organisations. While scientific communities have their own indicators and purposes, they are organised in parallel with policy and governmental agency, and are closely interlinked through necessity. While one wing talks of reliability and data inquiry, the other wing speaks of policy crises, financial management and elaborated systems. The creation of tables and charts, formed from numbers, always involved the world of imagination. This new cognitive space in education includes discoveries and relational ties, and often unacknowledged, invented and fabricated entities and associations. It describes and remakes in the task of inventing and legitimising the newly imagined world of education and its governance.

References

Desrosières, Alain (2002) *The Politics of Large Numbers: a history of statistical reasoning*, new edn, trans. Camille Naish. Boston, MA: Harvard University Press. (Originally published 1993, in French.)

Lawn, M. (2011) Governing through Data in English Education, *Education Inquiry*, 2(2), 277-288.

Lefebvre, H. (1991 [English trans.]) *The Production of Space*. Oxford: Blackwell.

Ozga, J., Dahler-Larsen, P., Segerholm, C. & Simola, H. (2011) *Fabricating Quality in Education – data and governance in Europe*. Abingdon: Routledge.

Porter, Theodore M. (1996) *Trust in Numbers: the pursuit of objectivity in science and public life*, new edn. Princeton: Princeton University Press.

Smyth, John A. (2008) The Origins of the International Standard Classification of Education, *Peabody Journal of Education*, 83(1), 5-40.

The Internationalization of Education Data: exhibitions, tests, standards and associations

MARTIN LAWN

SUMMARY Nation-states and their regions began to produce education data from the mid 1850s or thereabouts, often under pressure from the need to produce data for the World Exhibitions to accompany their displays. The growth of data – its range and depth – began in the twentieth century and reflected breakthroughs in testing and the related complex statistical operations used to manage and understand the resultant data. In some ways, the USA was the leader in this work but when international comparative projects began in the post-war period, newer entrants into the field created the leading edge. Governing education systems began to change and older administrative or agent-based evaluations were dislocated by the arrival of large-scale international surveys.

Throughout the twentieth century, the measurement of education became a defining element of the governing of education. At first, it was part of the accumulating physical resources of administrative offices, and usually recorded the budgetary elements, like the cost of teachers or population expansion costs. It could exist in centralized and decentralized sites, and even in non-linked offices. Then gradually, and especially since the 1950s, the amount of numerical data expanded, partly with the use of testing and selection, comparisons and productivity audits, and the rise of powerful digital technologies. Its uses grew exponentially, which allowed a new imaginary to grow in which this data provided new educational realities and landscapes, and eventually closely focused interventions and controls. The increasing use of numerical data was driven by the ability of its measuring tools to be standardized, which allowed the production of data to be reproduced across specialist research centres in many places, and secondly, by the demand of policy actors for effective support in managing educational crises. The governing of education systems is increasingly connected to the capacity of data servers, software developments and the use of data-mining tools.

In this chapter, significant cases in the increasing use of education data are explored. Firstly, the place of world exhibitions, fairs and congresses is marked, and in the case of education, the role of the United States in making data and not just objects central to its display of its progress. Secondly, the problems of creating data and its agents can be seen in the slow rate of increase of clear data in the United Kingdom, and lastly, the role of international associations, their experts and their attendant role in system governance is described.

The great exhibitions and scientific congresses of the nineteenth century fostered the growth of numerical data, which was used to aid comparisons between national education systems and to assist the spectacle of exhibitions and the arrival of the future.

> As early as the 1850s, statisticians in a number of European countries had come to recognize education as a field of statistical inquiry that could benefit from the exchange of professional experience among statisticians of different countries, as was beginning to happen in other more established fields of inquiry such as population statistics. Indeed, education was one of 11 branches or fields of statistics separately identified for discussion at the first International Statistical Congress held in Brussels in 1853, and it was featured from time to time in the programs of subsequent congresses up until the First World War. The International Statistical Institute (ISI), which assumed the responsibility for organizing these congresses, after it came into existence as a professional association of statisticians in 1885, took an active interest in this field, but the earliest studies were mostly single country studies. (Smyth, 2008, p. 7)

The growing authority of data in governing education systems in the twentieth century was greatly influenced by its use in the United States and its value in the world exhibitions to compare systems. The United States had created an agency to collect the annual reports of the State's education:

> the federal role in education expanded considerably with the creation of the Department of Education in 1867 (reorganized shortly afterward as the Bureau of Education). Many of the proponents of a federal department had hoped for a more active and influential institution, but the Congress created an agency mainly to collect and disseminate educational statistics. (Vinovskis, 1996, p. 113)

The collection of data was seen as a catalyst in the improvement of education:

State superintendents also used comparative school statistics to
shame educationally backward districts to improve their public
schools. (Vinovskis, 1996, p. 114)

Data was collected even though the rise of data was associated with the
expansion of the role of the federal government in state and local education.
(Vinovskis, 1996, p. 115)

By the time of the Paris Exposition in 1878, the United States was able
to produce many reports and tables about its education systems for display,
and in doing so, began to shape the future of comparison through the
exhibition medium. The nature and quality – even value – of the data
produced could act only as a guide to the American systems but its influence
went wider. It was seen as an exemplar. The aim was ambitious; it was
intended to represent the different grades and systems of education, its
materials and appliances of instruction and training, and the results attained
(Philbrick, 1878, p. 13).

Reporting to the New York Legislature, Bradley made great claims for
American data and its effects:

> Another respect in which the American exhibit surpassed all
> others was in the annual reports of State and city departments of
> education. No European country can show any such set of
> educational reports as Massachusetts exhibited. No European city
> has school reports which compare with those of Boston and St.
> Louis. Scarcely less worthy of commendation are the reports of
> the Board of Regents of this State. Models also in their way,
> although but a few volumes are yet published, are the annual
> reports of the United States Bureau of Education. These and
> other sets of reports constituted a body of educational literature
> which was a noteworthy feature of the United States exhibit.
> (Bradley, 1879, p. 121)

But the local States produced the collected data voluntarily; there was no
power of compulsion. The relative weakness of the overall data was arguably
a sign of the strength of the US system, as its annual production motivated
local States to treat data production competitively, and as a sign of their
superior organization. But, as Philbrick makes clear, the data was incomplete
and impressive only in its collection and not in its accuracy:

> One object in presenting the comparative view contained in these
> tables is to show the increasing completeness, from year to year, in
> the returns thus voluntarily furnished. It will be observed that in
> some items the returns are much more complete than in others;
> for example, while nearly every state and territory reports the
> 'number enrolled,' only twenty-seven out of the thirty-eight states
> report the 'number in daily attendance,' and this accounts in part
> for the great difference between those numbers. It will be observed

that the 'school population' is far greater than the number
enrolled; this difference is largely due to the fact, that in a majority
of the states 'school population' means the number of those
persons who are between six and twenty-one years old, which is
obviously a much larger number than could be expected to be
enrolled as pupils in schools. (Philbrick, 1878, p. 31)

Bradley rather overrode these problems with the data and made the kind of
claim which would become commonplace in comparison:

In one of the reports of the Commissioner of Education in the
United States Educational Exhibit at the Exposition, a large
collection of facts and statements of the observations and opinions
of superintendents of large manufacturing establishments is given,
from which it appears that a common school education adds fifty
per cent, and such an additional education as can be obtained in
most of our union schools and academies adds two hundred per
cent to the productiveness of the ordinary unskilled labourer.
(Bradley, 1879, p. 8)

With the rise in data came the problem of its display. Piles of reports and
tables did not produce the spectacular impression that models and complex
displays aimed for. Bradley was impressed in Paris by the London School
Board display, which showed:

a large map of London, giving the location of each school, and
showing all the central portions thickly dotted over with them, and
school buildings for 54,000 more children in process of erection in
the outskirts. (Bradley, 1879, p. 14)

It was simple but effective. Claims for the benefit of graphical displays, that
could store large amounts of data and where the viewer could see data
relations easily, were important to the exhibitions. These images of data were
seen as 'speaking for themselves' and offering an 'unmediated realism'
(Ekström, 2008 p. 36). Not only was statistical data to become standardized
but so too were the elements of graphical display, which then became part of
a new language within the exhibitions, a form of universal language which
spoke about society directly to the viewer.

In its construction, and in its representation, statistical data needed
standardization and national and international associations organized for this
purpose. Congresses were key parts of a process which agreed units of
measurement and methods of observation and experiment. Exhibitions had
begun the process of prioritizing displays of data, and testing new ways to
impress the visitor with these displays, but it was in a science linked to state
purposes that data pushed forward rapidly with forms of accurate
communication and standardized processes.

> Scientists ... militated for standards and greater accuracy in measurement. This was paramount for communication and comparability of research results. Equally important, scientific experimentation was grounded in instrumentation and the technology of instrumentation relied on standardization both for the internal operation of the device and for the definition and operationalization of the physical parameters under examination. (Crawford et al, 1993, p. 20)

The experts who worked in this field knew each other or knew of each other, even over great distances, by reputation and work, through the publication of experimental results or common problems. So, although they had particular sites of work, they inhabited a common scientific space. While tests did flow across borders into other systems of education, they did so with the assistance of the academics who produced them, and published, in books and journals, about them. This work could be replicated at a distance as it was based on the growth of standardized procedures. In a slow but discernible way, the publication in an American context of test results and standards of work 'travelled' across scientific communities, especially if the academic also travelled to American sites of work.

Eventually, it was almost impossible to conceive of schooling or the child except through the concepts and the proofs this community offered. Constant reference back across borders was usual in most policy debates, i.e. it was important to know that the science or the policy or the professoriate from elsewhere were behind the data or proposals.

The United States continued and strengthened its focus on education reporting in the early twentieth century, and measuring the education systems in the United States became a major activity (Callahan, 1962). The new field of education management, staffed by PhD graduates with statistical competence and an interest in measurement, had filled the space between managers and teachers. Using fieldwork, tests and surveys, they collected data on all aspects of the education system. Regional research laboratories were established across the United States and their staff spent their time in testing and standardizing units of measurement. The American efficiency movement in education produced data about everything from desks to children:

> We measure cost, teaching efficiency, progress through school, success in studies, mentality, buildings, equipment, textbooks and attendance by methods and devices almost unknown only a dozen years ago. (Sears, 1924, p. 137)

By the time of the New York World's Fair in 1939, the United States had become still more sophisticated in the production and display of its data. The New York State Department Research Division produced pages of simplified data, through the use of pictorial figures representing finance or distribution and use, over time. The point was to show the 'multitudinous and complex'

15

problems and costs of New York State education and 'For the layman to picture these problems as clearly as the expert can with his statistics' (New York State Education Department, 1939a, p. 1).

The publication *New York Learns* (New York State Education Department, 1939b), also produced for the World's Fair, used much of the same data but embedded it within narratives about the advances in the city and the necessity to educate the public about increased tax costs for educating each child as a personality and within his own capacity. Progressive methods and equipment cost more and there were already 625,000 culturally diverse elementary pupils, taught by a corps of more than 20,000 teachers. A narrative about opportunity and progressive experiment was based upon statistical data and institutional description. Both New York education data reports used within the New York World's Fair were constructed within the American tradition of detailed education reporting and were based upon numerical data, but they also faced the problem of persuasion and display, and solved it in different ways. It was no longer a question of data alone but of public explanation and persuasion.

UK History

The idea of collecting information regularly, like the American or 'Continental' systems, was not regarded as useful by the British at first. It was resisted. A senior official argued that it was necessary to collect information on costs, which was related to the distribution of grants, but useless to relate costs to results or products (Selby- Bigge, 1934, p. 65). So, the comparison of costs with those of other systems could produce only a 'general impression' of that system and was of little assistance in 'estimating the value' of British education (Selby-Bigge, 1934, p. 66). Although the Board of Education in Westminster, the main government office for education in England, reported annually on expenditure and estimates for the following year, there were problems in developing this further. Selby-Bigge, the main officer of the Board from 1911 to 1925, argued that the Board had limited resources for 'the extraction and appropriate tabulation of administrative data' and there were limits on the demands the Board could make for data upon the local authorities (Selby-Bigge, 1934, p. 220). In that period, and for a greater part of the twentieth century, it was the local education authorities which used administrative data for education because they were responsible for their local schools – for their establishment, management, and growth. Most of this data was not collected nationally, or even locally, in many cases.

The growth of statistics in education was related to the problems of a system local in its organization and responsibility. The central collection of data was always seen as politically threatening to the regions and counties, yet it was inexorable. The information collected was political and reflected new problematics; for example, when the (national) Board of Education collected data on the cost per child for elementary education in each local area in the 1920s, it did so because of huge variations in local provision. This was due to the local taxes for education and the resistance of local ratepayers (who were franchised by property) to having to pay for other people's children! As local taxes paid for the teachers, there were continuing disputes with organized teachers in many areas. Also, this reflects a growing responsibility at the centre for the quality of elementary education.

In 1964, the West Riding Education Committee, a local area of town and country in the north of England, produced a major report on its work for the years 1954 to 1964. Within it, numerical data was assembled from many different parts of the education service and was threaded through its narrative of progress. For example, over a 10-year period, figures were provided about the number of exchange students, agricultural students, Schools Museum Service film loans, youth groups, and school library service loans. The audience for the report was local, and it was recognized in the introduction that the report reflected a 'promise' and not a requirement. Although it is clear that a major effort had been taken to find as much quantitative information as possible, often from previously silent sources, it was primarily a narrative of administration. The task of creating data enabled a further stage to take place: analysis. It was possible to show what was happening to the school population; the rise and fall of primary and secondary pupil numbers, pass/fail exam rates, students leaving for university, and staffing numbers in schools. The report was able to show that its teacher training colleges were supplying teachers mainly to the south of England, at its cost. It could compare its costs of provision of salaries, premises, transport and equipment with 48 other counties and rank its performance. It could begin its own research projects, for instance on the cleaning of schools and the training of its school caretakers; floor sweepings were collected, weighed, measured, and sampled, and new methods used to clean schools. In this way, a narrative of progress was tethered and justified by the use of data. Comparisons could be made and inquiry undertaken. The local authority had begun to move out of administration and into a democratic accounting of its work. It was a leading education authority and needed to justify its actions and costs. Data was used to validate its work but could also be used to criticize its progress compared to others. Its display of its data was simple, given that it had been extracted from different services, and it had not yet reached the usefulness of the New York World's Fair data in the transparent ways that it was presented.

Scotland, a separate education system within the UK, tended to view the collection of statistical information about the country as a public and professional concern, so, in 1947, government departments were asked about the potential value for research purposes of the material which they collect and to suggest new methods and areas of collection.

The education research community formed a special committee for this purpose, which soon began to shape the collection of education statistics in

Scotland. To allow comparisons to be made, they wanted the same data to be collected and displayed in Scotland and England, i.e. the Scottish Education Department's Report, *Education in Scotland in 1948* and the statistical tables which form Part II of the corresponding Ministry of Education Report for England and Wales, *Education in 1948*. For example, they asked that a table should be published showing the number of classes of different sizes in various types of school; the age and date of birth of each pupil, to be taken from their birth certificate; and the official name of each school and the full postal address to be used. More requests of this nature followed. The accuracy of this data could then be used to produce precise information about the number of pupils, born in a given year, and their age distribution, from headline information in the class register. They required unambiguous data to show the distribution of teachers by sex, age, qualifications and school. In effect, what the head teachers and researchers wanted was clear state information which would allow them to make analyses about female/male teacher ratios or the rise or fall of teaching qualifications. They wanted a shift from administrative data, collected haphazardly and displayed without accuracy, that it was not possible to compare.

The new demand for clear and transparent information for comparable purposes, seen in Scotland, became a pressing issue for new post-war organizations. From the outset, the newly formed United Nations Educational, Scientific and Cultural Organization (UNESCO) had an obligation to collect and analyse statistics in education, which made it the 'premier education statistics institution' in the 1950s (Heyneman, 1999, p. 66). Its major problem was related to the definition and classification of key education terms, such as school, class and grade. Many discussions took place in the 1950s to try to resolve questions of definition and agree international standardization. Data could not be collected, and so allow analysis and comparison, unless it was clear what objects or processes were to be investigated. Heyneman quotes the 1955 UNESCO World Survey and illustrates a constant problem in the twentieth-century move to collect data:

> The table has many gaps and, even where figures are known, they
> are based on such varied procedures as to lack comparability ...
> The most complete measure of the education development of a
> country is to be found in the proportion of the child population
> actually attending school. This unfortunately, is rarely known.
> (p. 67)

Standardized key terms were also a problem: they had to be defined in a way that made sense across very different systems:

> A *grade* is a stage of instruction usually covered in the course of a
> school year.

> A class is a group of pupils (students) who are usually instructed
> together during a school term by a teacher or by several teachers.
> (Smyth, 2008, p. 22)

A *Manual of Educational Statistics* was published in 1961 aiming 'to explain suggested definitions, classifications and tabulations of educational statistics' (UNESCO, 1961, p. 8). With standardized national reporting established on an annual basis, the *Statistical Yearbook* (started in 1963) became UNESCO's main vehicle for the publication of international educational statistics (UNESCO, 1961, p. 28). So, by the 1960s, the value of data in the governing of education systems varied from bureaucratic data to research and policy data. Its presence varied from country to country. The direction was clear though. Collection, classification and standardization aided the movement of data across borders, and did so through international associations and projects. The governing of education systems became associated with the use of data.

Post-war European History

In post-war Europe, discussions about the collection and use of data began to take place through newly established specialist education centres, outside the national agencies, and by the creation of international associations. Quantitative researchers in education, using statistical techniques, and often trained as psychologists within an intelligence testing community, begin to work together, driven by the possibilities of European collaboration and data analysis. From simple meetings, powerful tools and projects were devised in the 1960s which became the basis for the governing of education by benchmarks and indicators.

From the 1950s, in post-war Europe, through post-war American policy in West Germany, the establishment of UNESCO and its Institutes of Education, and the growth of specialist research associations (which joined together embryo national research centres), the post-war world was assembled and locked together with an international infrastructure. In the 1940s and 1950s, a number of countries (the UK, Denmark, Norway, Sweden, Belgium, Finland, German Federal Republic) had set up commissions and organizations of varying degrees of independence concerned with the conduct and fostering of educational research directly concerned with policy making – for example, in Finland, the Centre for Educational Research at the University of Jyväskylä (a state-supported independent institute, founded in 1957, working on research design, and empirical investigations in national and international projects) (Takala, 1963) and in England, the National Foundation for Educational Research, an independent research organization founded in 1946, supported by local education authorities and teacher unions, which developed a strong presence in educational testing. National capacity in educational research, defined as quantitative and based on factorial analysis and testing methodologies, grew.

Individual national researchers with experience and skill were utilized, like Torsten Husén in Sweden, who had published major studies on pupils, ability and school performance, and from the United States leading quantitative researchers like Benjamin S. Bloom of the University of Chicago and Robert L. Thorndike of Teachers College, Columbia University. Sometimes, these network links depended upon key actors who had been international in their activity or research work pre-war (Lawn, 2008). As the national centres came into being, they were influenced by this international experience, particularly on selection for secondary education, and they acted as a wider European resource when opportunities occurred to do significant and policy-influenced research work. International scientific cooperation depended on the development of these research centres and their technical competence (a post-war phenomenon) (Wall, 1970). This network of centres and experts founded its own organization to develop international projects on school research, the International Association for the Evaluation of Educational Achievement (IEA). Being in the IEA had local effects as well: the Institute of Educational Research in Jyväskylä found that joining the IEA project helped to establish its position with the government and with the research community in Finland (Purves, 1987, p. 14) and a report on the Belgian centre described its local advantages as:

> definite techniques such as multi-stage sampling, multiple
> regression analysis, score weighing, etc. But it seems to me that
> even more important is that personal and work relations are
> created with leading scholars such as B.S. Bloom, R. Thorndike,
> J. Carroll, T. Husén, G. Peaker, and so many others, with
> directors of National Foundations for Educational Research, with
> national IEA project directors and technical officers. ... The
> amount of information, help, and advice thus made possible is
> invaluable. (Purves, 1987, p. 15)

In this way, the influence of data, and the skills needed to produce it, became more embedded in different countries by centres which were formally linked together and working in funded projects. International cooperation grew out of a scientific community and national policy needs but it was cultivated as part of a Cold War, in which education systems symbolized divergent international politics. The role of the United States in supporting and connecting scholars and centres was important in the 1950s, especially in conferences and projects, and in the demand for 'common methods and techniques, international scales and measuring instruments, and essential terminology in educational research' (Noll, 1958, p. 85). Administrative data collected for the purposes of funding systems and controlling costs, and represented in tabular form, began to be challenged in education by scientific project data, produced by statisticians and researchers. This data was treated dynamically. It fused the factorial analysis and empirical study methods of the psychologists with the concerns of comparativists in education with curriculum and school processes (Wall, 1979, p. 252). A professional community, the IEA, working nationally on local studies yet part of a wider scientific community, was encouraged by the problems of post-war Europe to extend the scope of its work in international and comparative study, funded by government. Data drawn from a range of international studies across the school curriculum, undertaken in the 1960s, had also produced 'a highly complex array of international and intercultural variables', with accurate measurements, 'by cross national comparison and sampling' (Wall, 1970, p. 497).

The basic idea of the founders of the IEA was that the world could be conceived as a huge educational laboratory (Husén, 1983, p. 26) where different national practices could lend themselves to comparisons that would yield new insights into the determinants of educational outcomes, serving as a basis for the improvement of the quality of education. It was felt that even to undertake a self-improvement audit of an educational system required a review of practices in other countries, providing a checklist of ideas and possible actions to help understand strengths and overcome weaknesses. This type of research, when applied to achievement outcomes, could lead to valid international standards.

In both cases, it was their work in science – agreeing measuring devices, conceptualizing systems, sharing data – that enabled them to work across borders, and influence education governance. Not only was the data conceived dynamically, but it was no longer trapped within printed reports and tables: the IEA decided to centralize the work of data processing in a Data Processing Centre, in order to be able to re-use and further expand knowledge gathered in the individual studies. This step was made necessary not only by the increasing number of IEA studies but also by the growing number of participating countries, which made the work of data processing more demanding.

The IEA, growing out of a collection of expert national researchers, and wanting to undertake interesting comparative projects in education at a high level, found itself in a familiar situation. Research steering and funding began to shape its activities more over time, and there was less concern with the researcher's interests in inquiry and more with the policy lessons of comparison.

> Although the initiative was still with the researchers who
> submitted proposals reflecting academic priorities, the growing
> number of requests for proposals on the part of the governmental
> agencies led to an increasing dependence on the grant-giving
> agencies with regard to the choice of research topics. (Husén
> 1983, p. 22)

While UNESCO concerned itself with the clarification of terms, the communication of data and country studies, the IEA undertook large-scale studies with larger and larger groups of countries. From the 1960s, governing education systems through research-based data became an essential component of the need for comparison, a key element itself in assessing productivity and efficiency. The arrival of the Organization for Economic Cooperation and Development (OECD) and its metamorphosis from a professional and economic organization tightened research/policy relations in Europe:

> The [OECD] was ... well placed to respond to the mounting pressure in the late eighties for a new intergovernmental effort to develop [educational performance] indicators. This pressure was, of course, directly related to the quality and accountability movements, but also to the prevailing fashion for international comparisons in an increasingly competitive world climate. (Papadopoulos, 1994, pp. 189-90)

Pressure from its major funder, the United States, intensified the gradual European movement towards strong research collaborations on broad policy issues into a much tighter direction towards cross-national comparisons. Although conceptually or technically or politically problematic, data had to be produced on the performance of entire systems. Direct pressure from the main funder, the United States, forced

> OECD to engage itself in a project collecting and analyzing statistical education 'inputs and outcomes' – information on curricular standards, costs and sources of finance, learning achievements on common subject matter, employment trends, and the like. (Heyneman, 1993, p. 375)

The United States had been moving in this direction, on performance data, since, in 1988, the US Office for Educational Research and Improvement (OERI) collected a group of state experts together to analyse the 'increasing interest' states have in 'developing, shaping and evaluating the success of schools' (OERI, 1988, p. 1). Indicators of performance, institutional competition, public data and accountability, and reporting systems became a new American norm, and through the OECD, a European norm. The science of measurement was shared across differing and asymmetrical policy contexts and slowly synchronized them.

International leadership in the production of education performance data moved to the OECD with the creation of its Programme for International Student Assessment (PISA) and away from UNESCO (Cusso & D'Amico, 2005, p. 207). The shift to indicators and benchmarking through the Open Method of Coordination within the European Union and the effects of the regular PISA assessments produced a way of steering education through data production:

> The publication of rankings of national education systems according, for example, to the results of PISA, brings out the close relationship between the international statistical evaluations and

the reform of education systems that has indirectly – or directly – been defended by OECD, the EU or the World Bank. (Cusso & D'Amico, 2005, pp. 210-211)

A close relation between the international statistical comparisons and the reform and steering of education policies had become established.

Dominant Flows: science and policy in education

Throughout the twentieth century, the measurement of education became a defining element in the governing of education. The driving force for this movement was twofold: firstly, the ability of measuring tools to be standardized and the production of data to be reproduced across specialist research centres, and secondly, the demand of policy actors for effective support in governing education systems under stress. Statistics provided legitimacy for, and a redefinition of social knowledge, and its tools and processes were actively used in administration and social reform in the twentieth century. It symbolized objectivity and rigour (Porter, 1995). It was taken to solve crises and became useful to the process of governing systems.

Education data was produced in democratic systems, at national or local level, to explain costs, organization and progress. In elite systems, data was not viewed as important as elite knowledge, and was therefore not numerical or publicly available. Data was used to explain the system, and its professionals often demanded data to understand the processes they had responsibility for. It had another useful function too; data tended to displace politics and its arguments. Numbers had power, for few knew the processes of their construction or what was elided or excluded. The few who knew worked increasingly together in post-war networks and projects.

In the last few decades, data has become key to the governing of education in several European states, and through international comparison, it has great discursive power across many education sites. No longer just administrative, it is now linked to performance, audit and production.

References

Bradley, J.E. (1879) Report to the Legislature of the State of New York on the Educational Exhibits at the Paris Exposition of 1878 and the Application of Art and Industry. Albany: Benthuysen.

Callahan, R.E. (1962) *Education and the Cult of Efficiency.* Chicago: University of Chicago Press.

Crawford, E., Shinn, T. & Sorlin, S. (Eds) (1993) *Denationalizing Science: the contexts of scientific practice.* Dordrecht: Kluwer.

Cusso, R. & D'Amico, S. (2005) From Development Comparatism to Globalization Comparativism: towards more normative international education statistics, *Comparative Education*, 41(2), 199-216.

Desrosières, A. (2003) Managing the Economy: the state, the market, and statistics, in T. Porter & D. Ross (Eds) *The Cambridge History of Science*. Vol. 7: *Modern Social and Behavioral Sciences*, pp. 553-564. Cambridge: Cambridge University Press.

Ekström, A. (2008) 'Showing at One View': Ferdinand Boberg's 'statistical machinery' and the visionary pedagogy of early twentieth-century statistical display, *Early Popular Visual Culture*, 6(1), 35-49.

Heyneman, S.P. (1993) Quantity, Quality, and Source, *Comparative Education Review*, 37(4), 372-388.

Heyneman, Stephen P. (1999) The Sad Story of UNESCO's Education Statistics, *International Journal of Educational Development*, 19(1), 65-74.

Husén, T. (1983) The International Context of Educational Research, *Oxford Review of Education*, 9(1), 21-29.

Lawn, M. (2008) *An Atlantic Crossing? The Work of the IEI, its Researchers, Methods and Influence*. Oxford: Symposium Books.

Ministry of Education (1948) *Education in 1948. Report for England and Wales.* Report of the Interdepartmental Committee on Social and Economic Research. Cmd. 7724. London: His Majesty's Stationery Office.

New York State Education Department (1939a) *A Generation of Education*. New York: State Education Department.

New York State Education Department (1939b) *New York Learns – a Guide to the Educational Facilities of the Metropolis*. New York: Barrows (American Guide Series), New York Federal Writers' Project.

Noll, V. (1958) International Cooperation in Educational Research, *International Review of Education*, 4(1), 77-87.

Office for Educational Research and Improvement (OERI) (1988) *Measuring Up: questions and answers about state roles in educational accountability*. Washington, DC: OERI.

Papadopoulos, G.S. (1994) *Education 1960-1990: the OECD perspective*. Paris: OECD.

Philbrick, J.D. (1878) *United States Exhibition of Education. The Catalogue of the United States Collective Exhibition of Education, Paris Universal Exposition*. London: Chiswick Press.

Porter, T. (1995) *Trust in Numbers*. Princeton: Princeton University Press.

Purves, A.C. (1987) The Evolution of the IEA: a memoir, *Comparative Education Review*, 31(1), Special Issue on the Second IEA Study, pp. 10-28.

Scottish Education Department (1949) *Education in Scotland in 1948. A Report of the Secretary of State for Scotland*. Cmd. 7656. Edinburgh: His Majesty's Stationery Office/

Sears, J.S. (1924) Development of Tests and Measurements, in I.L. Kandel (1924) *Twenty Five Years of American Education*, pp.117-139. New York: Macmillan.

Selby- Bigge, Sir L.A. (1934) *The Board of Education*, 2nd edn. London: Putnam.

Smyth, J.A. (2008) The Origins of the International Standard Classification of Education, *Peabody Journal of Education*, 83(1), 5-40.

Takala, M. (1963) The Organisation and Structure of Secondary Education, *International Review of Education*, 9(2), 236-240.

UNESCO (1961) *Manual of Educational Statistics*. Paris: UNESCO.

Vinovskis, M.A. (1996) The Changing Role of the Federal Government in Educational Research and Statistics, *History of Education Quarterly*, 36(2), 111-128.

Wall, W.D. (1970) Research and Educational Action, International Review of Education, 16(4), 484-501.

Wall, W.D. (1979) Psychology of Education, *International Review of Education – Internationale Zeitschrift fftr Erziehungswissenschaft – Revue internationale de pedagogie*, XXV, 367-391.

Policing Validity and Reliability: expertise, data accumulation and data parallelisation in Bavaria, 1873-1919

MARCELO CARUSO

SUMMARY Data becomes particularly 'informative' when actors consider validity and reliability as given facts. In this contribution, the disputes over these two dimensions of 'data' are credited as being major forces in its exponential growth. In the context of power struggles between emerging professional groups, liberal governance, and cleric school inspectors, the multiplication of data in the Kingdom of Bavaria during the Second Empire was an outcome of challenged legitimacies. This resulted in the parallelisation of processes of data collection and accumulation and, correspondingly, in a major drive towards the growth of data.

Before educational research became involved in producing data on education, educational administrations were the most important agents for the growth of educational data. The nineteenth century was marked by the emergence of large administrative apparatuses in the field of education, which opened up an unprecedented path in data production and accumulation regarding education and schools. It was not only in this respect that German states in the nineteenth century were the forerunners in this development. As early as the late eighteenth century, German states, not only Prussia and Bavaria, but also smaller states and even city states, had initiated comprehensive rounds of data collection and systematisation. For instance, the first appointed official for school reform in Prussia, Karl Abraham von Zedlitz (1731-93), organised an extensive survey of all Prussian schools and, in doing so, laid the groundwork for an intended educational reform. In a highly fragmentary state such as Prussia, building an 'educational state' was equated with a consistent policy of data production and flow at this early stage of development (Heinemann, 1974; Schleunes, 1989).

Yet educational data, if it is expected to exceed the mere status of ritual collection and to become the basis for educational governance, is a highly cultural construction. The power of data heavily relies on a belief in its validity – a correspondence between the data and the reality being described and constructed through data production – and reliability – the consistency of a measure as an indicator of the objectivity and lack of bias of the data collector. Beyond statistics, validity and reliability are considered here as social processes. They involve both a suitable approach to reality – commonly based on some form of 'expert knowledge' – leading to a more or less appropriate and reasonable production of data, and a steadiness of measurement and judgement from using different data collectors to avoid the risk of distorting data. As social processes, the validity and reliability of data are highly dependent upon issues such as attributing expertise and trust. Recent discussions concerning evidence-based policies are only possible in a setting in which these two key elements in producing social prestige and cultural authority – expertise and trust – are clearly assets of the actors involved in these kinds of proposal (Boyer, 2008; Ash, 2010).

In the following, I will focus on a particular situation of contested expertise and limited trust that eventually led to the growth of educational data: the discussions on and transformation of data-producing architectures in the Kingdom of Bavaria during the last decades of the nineteenth and the first decades of the twentieth centuries. The analysis of the Bavarian case will show that the growth of educational data, far from being a linear process of accumulation, improvement and refinement, displays the intriguing dynamics of cultural and political pluralisation, constructing different forms of educational information.

For this purpose, I will outline the first wave of institutionalisation of data collection and evaluation at the beginning of the nineteenth century. Then, I will present discussions and practices related to de-legitimising the reliability of information that resulted in a crisis in the expert status of school inspectors. In a third step, I will address the extension of this crisis of the group in charge of data production by showing how de-legitimising the validity of the data available eventually led to a crisis of confidence. In my conclusions, I will argue for an understanding of the growth of educational data as a social process combining competing forms of knowledge and processes of legitimate agency.

Institutionalising Data Collection
by Means of Inspection in Bavaria

At the turn of the nineteenth century, Bavarian elites embarked on an institutionalisation of elementary schooling. The most salient element of this strategy was the introduction of six-year compulsory schooling in 1802 (Liedtke, 1991, pp. 14, 42). In a time of consistent reformist zeal in the spirit of enlightened absolutism, this measure followed a wider pattern of dealing with social conflict and rural unrest in Central Europe that put school attendance as a key element in a strategy of governing populations (van Horn Melton, 1988). Yet the full significance of compulsive schooling within a strategy of social integration only developed when Bavaria achieved the status of a veritable kingdom in 1806 and incorporated Swabian and Franconian territories thanks to Napoleon's decisive support. It is in the new situation of integrating different 'ethnic' identities, dialects and political allegiances that popular schooling definitively became a privileged field of state-building and a symbol of the efficacy of the new polity (Hartmann, 1989).

It is not unexpected that, in the context of consolidating territorial borders, a spatially comprehensive strategy for the policing of schooling gained momentum (Zimmermann, 1996). Although educational motives may also have played a role in the decision to establish a system of school inspectorates in all parts of the kingdom, ignoring existing structures of school governance, the significance of the territorial challenges of the time was decisive here. The groundwork for this strategy had been laid as early as 1802 with the creation of a central department for schools within the Ministry of the Interior. A general curriculum inspired by Pestalozzi soon followed (1804), including some innovations such as object lessons. These regulations, together with some conservative changes stressing 'spiritual' lessons introduced in 1811, remained formally as the content basis for all Bavarian elementary schools (*Werktagsschulen, Volksschulen*) until 1926 (Welch, 1998).

For the reform elites, this drive to central regulation required establishing a pervasive chain of state authority dedicated to a specific control of schooling and to the flow of data related to this task. In the Bavarian constitution of 1808, the territory was divided into regions along 'ethnic' lines and each of these regions became a specific bureau for inspecting and controlling schools (Liedtke, 1991). Nonetheless, the masterpiece in the strategy of consolidating a new territoriality in the field of schooling was the general regulation for district and local inspectorates adopted on 15 September 1808. This document introduced two additional levels of school inspection and data production into the old and new parts of the kingdom. The first one, the district school inspectorates, became the 'direct auxiliary institution' of the regional officials in charge of schooling, and were also intended to help improve 'the inner state of all schools of their district'. The second one, the local school inspectors, also had to improve the quality of schooling and, at the same time, to focus on school discipline and teacher decorum (see 'Amts-Instruktion für die Distrikts-Schulinspektoren vom 15. September 1808' and 'Amts-Instruktion für die Lokal-Schulinspektoren vom 15. September 1808', both printed in Seiler, 1903, pp. 367-368, 373). A crucial aspect in this story was the role played by local school inspectors in guaranteeing a regular transfer of information to the different levels of the administration up to the Ministry in Munich. Mirroring the crucial role clergymen played in the production of educational knowledge in the German states (Caruso, 2003, pp. 96-108; Brachmann, 2008), almost all these inspectors were churchmen commissioned by the state authorities. Nevertheless, the inclusion of churchmen in key positions of the new mass schooling system did not mean rendering schools to the Churches because these churchmen operated explicitly as state agents. Scholars have usually agreed on the pragmatic character of this decision and it has been widely portrayed as the only way of guaranteeing pervasive control even in rural areas (Neukum, 1964, p. 21; Blessing, 1982, p. 32). With this organisational device, Bavarian mass schools expanded and reached an astonishing level of institutionalisation. The school inspectors regularly delivered the requested forms with rather detailed information concerning the state of the schools.

Yet what, at the beginning of the nineteenth century, may have been a pragmatic decision gained a clearly more ideological and political connotation in the second half of the nineteenth century. Regardless of its results in the consolidation of mass schooling (Siebenpfeiffer, 1830; Himmelstein, 1859), clerical school inspection struck a note of discord in the political and cultural struggles between liberal and conservative forces. Furthermore, the definitive organisation of the dominant Catholic-conservative Bavarian party and its rural basis only took place after 1867 in the context of a heated discussion concerning a new general law for elementary education that would have loosened the traditional ties between inspector positions and churchmen (Stache, 1981; Eichenlaub, 1989). In addition, liberal forces radicalised their positions during this time, and demanded churchmen to be consistently separated from the business of school inspection. Although well-known churchmen and school administrators had paved the way in the first half of the nineteenth century for a more 'specialised' or 'professional' handling of the information being collected in the inspection travels organised in the whole kingdom once a year, the legitimacy of their data and judgements came under sharp scrutiny during the Bavarian version of the *Kulturkampf* (Grasser, 1967).

After 1870, the almost uncontested appreciation of regional inspectors like the Lutheran preacher Heinrich Stephani (1761-1850), who undoubtedly had been the main innovative actor of school reform in Franconia between 1808 and 1834 (Stephani, 1835), waned considerably. New divisive lines emerged during the period up until 1890 that decisively changed the constellation of forces around the issue of school inspection. Whereas liberals and conservatives – most of them Catholics – voiced predictable positions regarding the participation of clergymen in controlling schools, a strategic shift among state bureaucrats, usually portrayed as moderate liberals, now favouring the implementation of alternative modes of inspection and control, changed the rules of the game. The traditional alliance between state officials and clergymen eroded dramatically in the political arena, regardless of the different ties still effective at local and regional levels. From 1873 onwards, new regional inspectors, all of whom were professional educators independent from the Churches, were appointed for the task of inspection and data collection and presentation. In addition, in many of the major cities of the kingdom, new school superintendents and inspectors replaced the old clerical ones (Caruso, 2003, pp. 121-150). In the rural regions, however, the clerical inspectors who were still operating had to work together with the new ones, and even in the cities clerics had to supervise the teaching of religion. The duality of this structure of data collection and presentation – simultaneous reports by clerical and professional inspectors – would persist until the brief Soviet experiment that Bavaria experienced in 1918 and 1919. The decision made by state officials, favouring non-clerical personnel for the task of inspection and data production after 1870, occurred in a specific context, namely a loss of legitimacy with regard to the traditional data collected by the clerics.

Reliability and Knowledge as Controversial Issues

Beyond the political conflict emerging over the proposed law for elementary schooling of 1869, traditional practices of data collection had come under sharp scrutiny even before this political controversy was unleashed. The first doubts with regard to the objectiveness of the data circulating in the administration arose when other officials began to inspect schools from 1867 onwards (for instance, see State Archive Bamberg, Regierung, K3/DII, 893). Suddenly, inspectors were coming twice in a school year, once with a cleric in charge and the other time with an administrator. The first dissonances emerged in this new context. The administration's response to these initial inconsistencies was to make the parallel inspections permanent by appointing regional professional inspectors in the seven regional governments.

At first sight, the assignment of new lay inspectors conducting inspections in parallel to the regular ones conducted by churchmen from 1873 onwards represented an attempt to test data reliability by means of parallelisation at the level of administrative practices. The administration believed the clerical inspectors were delivering inaccurate data as a result of inadequate professional preparation, or due to pressure from further pastoral obligations. Regional inspectors were not expected to replace the district and local clerical school inspectors, but rather to help the clerical inspectors to do their job more professionally. However, the spread of parallelisation in data production and flow revealed that the situation was even worse.

Bavarian archives have preserved numerous documents showing a disparate reality among the schools. I will now focus on some informational inconsistencies in a rural district, Schrobenhausen in Upper Bavaria, in order to illustrate this problem. In the village of Aresing, the contrast between the forms completed by the clerical and the non-clerical inspectors evidences a complete lack of data reliability. In May 1869, the district school inspector characterised the 'method' of the teacher as 'very good' and wrote, 'it was particularly pleasant to hear how the children read with understanding and the right emphasis' (inspections held on 10 May 1869 and 26 April 1870;

31

administrative decision of 8 January 1870, State Archive Munich, Schulämter 66). The district official who inspected the school a few months later highlighted the fact that the schoolchildren did not understand what they read and this put the 'method' in an unfavourable light. Only after this intervention from 'outside' did the district school inspector admonish the schoolteacher to pay attention to the comprehension of texts used in reading lessons (Report of the Inspector, May 1870, State Archive Munich, Schulämter 66). Again, the clerical district school inspector praised the 'very good' method at this school in 1880 and characterised it as 'a school as a school should be, conducted in a fatherly manner'; a few months later, the regional school inspector listed a number of problems in the methods used by the schoolteacher and criticised the children's lack of independence in writing, arithmetic and reading, thereby giving the school 'conducted in a fatherly manner' a negative connotation (inspection held on 21 April 1880; administrative decision of 20 August 1881, State Archive Munich, Schulämter 66). Similar discrepancies emerged repeatedly in the neighbouring village of Hörzhausen. In the school inspection form of 27 April 1883 the inspector commented that 'the children answer so freshly and pleasantly that it is a delight to hear them'. The same schoolteacher, in the eyes of the regional school inspector two years later, 'lacks self-control when he dialogues with the children: he poses numerous unnecessary questions ... ; the repetition of meaningless questions negatively affects the attention of the school children' (inspection held on 27 April 1883; administrative decision of 9 March 1885, State Archive Munich, Schulämter 103).

These discrepancies were by no means exceptions. The differences between the data produced by the district and local inspectors, on the one hand, and the professional regional inspectors, on the other, were consistently inconsistent. The first regional inspector of Middle Franconia (Nuremberg), Johann Methsieder, made his point against the value of the clerical data by contrasting judgements expressed in numbers. The general regulation for school inspection foresaw that inspectors had to give marks to all schools, school classes and teachers once a year. Whereas clerical school inspectors were quite generous in giving marks and producing positive data about schools, the work of the new regional inspectors produced more differentiated data. Whereas the clerical inspectors almost only knew the two best marks (I and II), Methsieder in Franconia began to differentiate the marks and distributed them in a statistically more 'convincing' way: I (2 schools, or school classes), I-II (9), II-I (25), II (18), II-III (37), III-II (8), III (14), III-IV (16), IV-III (none) and IV (1) ('Visitationen des Kreisschulinspektors pro 1874', 30 January 1874, State Archive Nuremberg, Regierung, KDI, Abgabe 1932, Titel XIII, 1672). To the eye of a statistician, the 'normal' distribution of these marks in Methsieder's reports could have been quite acceptable, contrary to the discretionary use of these marks by the clerical school inspectors (further discrepancies: 'Visitationen des K. Kreisschulinspektors pro 1877', State Archive Nuremberg, Regierung,

KDI, Abgabe 1932, Titel XIII, 1734). Against this background, it is not surprising that the regional school council in Upper Bavaria in 1876 intended to police the reliability of the school inspections by ordering an inspection by clerical inspectors in those school classes already visited by the new professional regional inspectors (report of the regional school council of Upper Bavaria of 6 April 1876, State Archive Munich, RA 53666).

The reaction to this policing of data reliability – the idea that two observers should come to a similar judgement – varied. In 1873, the local school inspector at the village of Inning in Upper Bavaria, a cleric, made a request for conducting unannounced inspections in addition to the ordinary one, 'because it is well known that an ordinary visitation can only be effective if it has been complemented by an unannounced inspection' (request of the district school inspector Scheidl in Inning, 13 November 1873, State Archive Munich, RA 53666). However, the overwhelming majority of the clerical inspectors, and virtually all the Catholic ones, reacted very negatively to this challenge. The local school inspector in Stier, Middle Franconia, complained that the rather negative data produced by the regional school inspector was impossible, because he had visited schools over the last seven years and knew his business very well. The only explanation he could offer for the discrepancy was the regional school inspector's open hostility towards clergymen. If the regional inspector were to continue to de-legitimise the authority of the clerical inspectors, 'a new year 48' – alluding to the European revolutions of 1848 – 'would come' (letter from the local school inspector in Stier, 27 August 1877, State Archive Nuremberg, Regierung, KDI, Abgabe 1932, Titel XIII, 1734). In the same vein, clerical inspectors warned against the 'double visitations' being installed (statement of the district inspectors from Pfaffenhofen an der Ilm, N°15388, approx. 1895, State Archive Munich, RA 53667).

Indeed, the defensive attitude of the clerical inspectors was successful in avoiding a complete professionalisation of data production and collection by means of other inspections. Nonetheless, discussions surrounding the inconsistencies eroded the cultural authority of the clerics, who had hitherto been considered as 'experts' in the field of elementary and popular schooling (for new professional authorities, see Caruso, 2009b). On the whole, the issue of reliability remained largely unsolved. The view that clergymen were generally incapable of enacting innovations in schooling gradually prevailed over the course of time. This first form of critique persisted for decades and led to an agonising attempt to improve the inspectors' didactic knowledge by organising specific further educational training for them after 1910 (Bavarian State Archive, MK 23011). Complaints that some inspectors did not know enough about the different teaching methods in each school subject to be able to fill in the forms correctly was largely attributed to their ignorance of such subjects. In this sense, the lack of reliability shook the expert status that the clerical inspectors had held. This deficiency could even be gauged by some quantifiable data, such as the marks that expressed the general state of a class or school. And this was irrespective of how well organised the statistical parts of the educational data had been since 1873, when the Central Bureau for Statistics in Munich had centralised the standardisation and compilation of statistical materials related to schools and education (circular from the regional government of Upper Bavaria to the districts, 2 April 1873, State Archive Munich, RA 53843). The main problem remained that the district school inspectors were not able 'to infer reliably with regard to the quality of teaching from students' answers and performance' because this cannot be learnt in books, but only from working as a schoolteacher (consultations in the regional school council in Middle Franconia, 1 February 1906, N°35997, State Archive Nuremberg, Regierung, KDI, Abgabe 1968, Titel XIII, 3804). A widespread sense that the available data under general quantitative information was of poor value, together with curricular and methodical issues (Caruso, 2009a), characterised educational discussions at the turn of the century.

Validity and Trust as Controversial Issues

The claim that the value of available data was low due to the inexperience of clerics in teaching and conducting schools was a benevolent one (Sterner, 1882). Another question arose from the parallelisation of data production from 1873 onwards. Discretionary practices became visible, practices that were not the result of a lack of knowledge, but rather of traditional local alliances distorting the value of data. The critique against clerical school inspectors was also directed at the credibility of these agents. The problem of educational data was not only that two different inspectors could come to different judgements, a problem that could be addressed by a more focused training of the clerics in school matters. It was also that inspectors were no longer credited as acting in a trustworthy manner. This last accusation weakened any trust in the validity of the information being produced by the clerical inspectors: educational data was not inconsistent because the inspectors were unable to inspect a school in a professional manner, but because they did not wish to do so.

The discretional handling of data by Catholic churchmen was a particularly alarming signal for state authorities. Suspicions concerning the objectiveness of data collected by these inspectors were frequent and explicit. The regional inspectors of the Upper Palatinate wondered in 1909 why all schools conducted by order sisters of the Catholic Church scored among the best in the region: 'The work of these sisters may be very eager; yet they cannot leave their mechanical way of teaching with all its rote learning. It should be the duty of the inspectors to adamantly override this mode of teaching contrary to regulations' ('Niederschrift über die Verhandlungen der Kreisschulkommission für den Regierungsbezirk der Oberpfalz und von Regensburg in der Sitzung vom 16. Dezember 1909', p. 13, State Archive Munich, RA 53905). These comments by the regional officials showed that the work of the clerical inspectors was 'contrary to regulations', an accusation of considerable importance addressed to clerics working for the state.

In the early twentieth century in particular, critics raised the question of the validity of the data being collected. The Upper Bavarian regional government criticised clerical school inspectors for refusing to consider '2' as the 'normal mark' during their visits: 'This is all the more regrettable because the use of a lenient norm reinforces the tendency of the schoolteachers to overestimate the results of their own teaching and no clear distinction can be drawn between good and inadequate achievements' ('Niederschrift über die Verhandlungen der Kreisschulkommission von Oberbayern am 7. Dezember 1907', p. 22, State Archive Munich, RA 53979/1). This uneasiness with the quality of data also dominated in the Palatinate. When the regional inspectors Roth and Zickgraf presented their results summarising regular school inspections by district and local school inspectors – only 4 out of 2513 school classes produced unsatisfactory results –, they commented that the norm appeared to be lenient, thus 'the real state of teaching is surely quite a different one' ('Protokoll, aufgenommen am 9. Dezember 1908 im Kollegialsitzungssaale der k. Regierung der Pfalz in Speyer', pp. 13-14, State Archive Munich, RA 53904). The regional inspector of the Upper Palatinate made unmistakably sharp remarks when presenting the results of the inspections in 1907: the average of all marks assigned by the clerical inspectors was 1.6 and 'the female school classes directed by sisters of the Catholic orders, almost without exception, received the best marks, similarly to all schools in the city of Regensburg, which only know very good teaching results' ('Niederschrift der Verhandlungen der Kreisschulkommission für den Regierungsbezirk der Oberpfalz und von Regensburg in der Sitzung vom 21. Dezember 1908', p. 12, State Archive Munich, RA 53904). In addition to his ironic comment, the brief remarks left on this report by one of the regional school inspectors in Upper Bavaria, Klaus Brixle, reveals the widespread mistrust regarding the data collected by the religious school inspectors at local and district levels.

Not only customs and leniency, but also plain cheating, became an issue when discussing the value of educational data. For instance, the regional inspector of the Upper Palatinate, Eugen Leipold (1847-1926), witnessed situations in which the local inspector lied to him in order to protect an old local schoolteacher (Leipold, 1912, pp. 86-87). In Upper Franconia, the regional officials observed how 'the children showed very poor performances when the regional inspectors spontaneously proposed a topic for a written composition' ('Niederschrift der Verhandlungen der Kreisschulkommission für Oberfranken in der ordentlichen Jahressitzung vom 26. November 1913', p. 10, State Archive Munich, RA 53904). The secular school inspector of the city of Bamberg conjectured that schoolteachers and local clerical inspectors came to an arrangement concerning which topics were to be practised in written composition ('Niederschrift der Verhandlungen der Kreisschulkommission für

Oberfranken in der ordentlichen Jahressitzung vom 26. November 1913', p. 13, State Archive Munich, RA 53904). Similarly, the regional inspector of the Palatinate, Wittmann, observed that there were more 'disciplinary procedures' against schoolteachers when more unannounced inspections by regional inspectors were carried out. In his eyes, this was definite proof of the distorted image of the Bavarian school system suggested by the regular school inspection ('Ordentliche Jahressitzung der Kreisschulkommission der Pfalz. Protokoll aufgenommen am 26. November 1909', p. 27, State Archive Munich, RA 53905).

Indeed, clerics were embedded in local networks and even dubious complicities. They often used indulgence and leniency in state matters as effective techniques of power in order to ensure local obedience and support. This was the case for some clerical school inspectors in Upper Franconia who were particularly generous in awarding marks to teachers in 1916. They argued that these marks had to take into consideration the wartime situation with all its deprivations. The regional government had to publish a circular highlighting the rule that 'in giving marks for teaching results, only the question of whether the performance of the students corresponded to the requirements of the curriculum' was to be considered ('Darstellung über den Stand des oberfränkischen Volksschulwesens, inbesondere über die seitens der K.-Regierung auf die Schulprüfungsverhandlungen ergangenen Bescheide', p. 5, State Archive Munich, RA 53904). These scenes of discretional information production and flow suggested that all efforts launched by the state in controlling and reforming elementary schooling would be in vain, if the validity of data were not to be restored (Muggenthaler, 1899).

While the parallelisation of data following the introduction of regional school inspectors had resulted in a widespread sceptical view concerning the reliability of educational data being produced in the kingdom, it had also led to a more crucial mistrust of the good faith of clerics as state agents. If the reliability discussion had questioned the expert status of the clerics, now the picturing of this group as untrustworthy, on account of the evidence provided by the system of parallelisation in the information production and flow, was tantamount to a deserved death toll to the authority of this group. An apparent loss of trust in the former capital these churchmen had constituted resulted in a crisis in the system of traditional inspection.

Data Parallelisation and the Growth of Data

After the turn of the century, political and pedagogical criticism against the inherited clerical school inspection system gained momentum (Beyhl, 1902). Even in a conservative stronghold such as the Upper Palatinate, officials were unambiguous when characterising the state of affairs: 'The old system of visitations constitutes a real obstacle for the children's education ... and tends to give an inaccurate image of the state of the school' ('Protokoll über die

Verhandlungen der Kreisschulkommission für Oberpfalz und Regensburg in der Sitzung vom 16. Dezember 1907', p. 6, State Archive Munich, RA 53904). The die had definitely been cast against clerical school inspection. Nonetheless, the path towards this change proved to be rather long. Not until 1909 were standardised forms for data collection revised in a direction more in tune with the new pedagogical imperatives and it required an additional 10 years to abolish the old system. Public ceremonies accompanied the visit of the school inspector.

Mistrust and the loss of legitimacy of a once solid and steady inspection system resulted in a closer policing of reliability and validity as crucial dimensions of data. In the long term, the parallelisation of school inspection, by casting a second glance at the inherited system and checking it for reliable information, demonstrated a clear disparity in the quality of information. When professional inspectors came to a village, their judgement of local schools varied greatly, whereas clerical inspectors were lenient – or even plainly dishonest – when gathering substantial data on the state of schools. How to determine the outcome of teaching remained a highly disputed issue. In addition to abolishing the most ceremonial aspects of the scene of data collection in 1909 (Bock, 1991), the question of which practices could deliver an insightful diagnosis of the results proved particularly controversial in the dual structure of data collection. The regional inspector of the Palatinate, Wittmann, recommended directly interrogating students in addition to different written exercises in order to break the influence of local clerics and their reports ('Niederschrift über die Konferenz der Distriktsschulinspektoren und Stadtschulreferenten der Pfalz', N°2591, 18 April 1914, Bavarian State Archive, MK 22863, attachment, p. 17).

The information's lack of validity brought to the fore the question of how trustworthy clerics were who were more strongly attached to local arrangements than to any rigorous process of valid data collection. As a result, educational data multiplied as an additional arena for defining the power of regulating schools. One district school inspector in Upper Bavaria criticised how he had to complete so many documents following a curriculum reform in the region in 1890, that he experienced a veritable 'inundation of information' (*Informationsflut*) to the extent that 'our ears tremble' (answer from the district inspector in Erding to the request of the district administration, 15 August 1895, State Archive Munich, RA 53667).

In the case of Bavaria, a noticeable growth in educational data from 1870 onwards was clearly neither the outcome of any pedagogical 'progress' attracting attention to further aspects of schooling, nor the product of any 'need' for such information for daily work in schools. Data growth reflected and reinforced the political struggle for legitimacy in the school system by confronting two forms of knowledge and two processes of producing legitimacy with each other. On the one hand, the inherited system of clerical inspection preferred a more formal approach to schooling and sought a minimal level of compliance with state regulations. Data obtained from these practices had a strong ritual value because it was the outcome of a negotiation between local actors and their limitations and the mediating – and sometimes protective – role of the clerics (Blessing, 1979). It was a form of knowledge and a strategy for constructing legitimacy closely related to producing acceptance on both sides, i.e. local communities and government officials. Liberals fought against this more ritual, ceremonial and consensual form of knowledge and legitimacy, and advocated knowledge which had only been subjected to 'realities' so defined by the emerging experts among the schoolteachers and officials. Now knowledge and legitimacy were no longer related to local voices and situations, but had to grapple with the new imperative of objective information preferred by liberals and bureaucrats. In this sense, the growth of educational data became a source and, at the same time, an outcome of political struggles of the nineteenth century related to the institutionalisation of mass schooling in Europe. Before scientists entered decisively into the field of producing educational data in the twentieth century, questions of validity and reliability had already become objects of policing.

References

Ash, M.G. (2010) Wissenschaft und Politik. Eine Beziehungsgeschichte des 20. Jahrhunderts, *Archiv für Sozialgeschichte*, 50, 11-46.

Beyhl, J. (1902) *Die Befreiung der Volksschullehrer aus der geistlichen Herrschaft*. Berlin: Buchverlag der 'Hilfe'.

Blessing, W. (1979) Umwelt und Mentalität im ländlichen Bayern. Eine Skizze zum Alltagswandel im 19. Jahrhundert, *Archiv für Sozialgeschichte*, 19, 1-42.

Blessing, W. (1982) *Staat und Kirche in der Gesellschaft. Institutionelle Autorität und mentaler Wandel in Bayern während des 19. Jahrhunderts*. Göttingen: Vadenhoeck & Rupprecht.

Bock, I. (1991) Das Schulwesen von 1871-1918. Gesamtdarstellung, in M. Liedtke (Ed.) *Handbuch der Geschichte des Bayerischen Bildungswesens*, vol. II, pp. 395-463. Bad Heilbrunn/Obb.: Klinkhardt.

Boyer, D. (2008) Thinking through the Anthropology of Experts, *Anthropology in Action*, 15(2), 38-46.

Brachmann, J. (2008) *Der pädagogische Diskurs der Sattelzeit. Eine Kommunikationsgeschichte*. Bad Heilbrunn/Obb.: Klinkhardt.

Caruso, M. (2003) *Biopolitik im Klassenzimmer. Zur Ordnung der Führungspraktiken in den Bayerischen Volksschulen (1869-1918)*. Weinheim: Beltz.

Caruso, M. (2009a) Enthemmung als Führungsstrategie. Transformationen der Unterrichtskultur in München an der Wende zum 20. Jahrhundert, *Zeitschrift für Pädagogik*, 55(3), 334-344.

Caruso, M. (2009b) Liberal Governance and the Making of Hierarchies: Oberlehrer in Munich's elementary schools (1871-1918), *Journal of Educational Administration and History*, 41(3), 223-238.

Eichenlaub, K. (1989) *Der Bayerische Schulgesetzentwurf von 1867*. Hildesheim: Olms.

Grasser, W. (1967) *Johann Freiherr von Lutz. Eine politische Biographie*. Munich: Stadtarchiv.

Hartmann, P.C. (1989) *Bayerns Weg in die Gegenwart. Vom Stammesherzogtum zum Freistaat heute*. Regensburg: Friedrich Pustet.

Heinemann, M. (1974) *Schule im Vorfeld der Verwaltung. Die Entwicklung der preußischen Unterrichtsverwaltung von 1771-1800*. Göttingen: Vandenhoeck & Ruprecht.

Himmelstein, F.X. (1859) *Das deutsche Schulwesen im Königreiche Bayern*. Würzburg: Verlag der Stahel'schen Buch- und Kunsthandlung.

Leipold, E. (1912) *Erinnerungen aus meinem Leben*. Regensburg: Manz.

Liedtke, M. (1991) Von der erneurten Verordnung der Unterrichtspflicht (1802) bis 1870. Gesamtdarstellung, in M. Liedtke (Ed.) *Handbuch der Geschichte des Bayerischen Bildungswesens*, vol. II, pp. 11-133. Bad Heilbrunn/Obb.: Klinkhardt.

Muggenthaler, M. (1899) *Handbuch des bayerischen Volksschulwesens*. Passau: Abt.

Neukum, J. (1964) Die volksschulpolitischen Bestrebungen in Bayern, 1818-1848. Ein Beitrag zur bayerischen Schulgeschichte. PhD thesis, Universität Erlangen-Nürnberg.

Schleunes, K.A. (1989) *Schooling and Society. The Politics of Education in Prussia and Bavaria, 1750-1900*. Oxford: Berg.

Seiler, G. (1903) *Schulbedarfgesetz vom 28. Juli 1902 mit Einleitung, Erläuterungen und Vollzugsvorschriften*. Munich: Beck.

Siebenpfeiffer, D. (1830) Unterricht (Träume, welche wirklich werden mögen), *Rheinbayern, eine vergleichende Zeitschrift für Verfassung, Gesetzgebung, Justizpflege, gesammte Verwaltung und Volksleben*, 1, 73-103.

Stache, C. (1981) *Bürgerlicher Liberalismus und katholischer Konservatismus in Bayern, 1867-1871*. Frankfurt/M.: Peter Lang.

Stephani, H. (1835) *Handbuch der Unterrichtskunst nach der bildenden Methode für Volksschullehrer*. Erlangen: Palm'schen Verlagsbuchhandlung.

Sterner, M. (1882) *Die Methodik der Volksschule unter Berücksichtigung der Schulhygiene und Schulzucht*. Straubing: Attenkofer.

van Horn Melton, J. (1988) *Absolutism and the Eighteenth-Century Origins of Compulsory Schooling in Prussia and Austria*. Cambridge: Cambridge University Press.

Welch, S. (1998) *Subjects or Citizens? Elementary School Policy and Practice in Bavaria 1800-1918*. Melbourne: University of Melbourne Press.

Zimmermann, C. (1996) Reformkontinuitäten im Schulsystem. Süddeutschland im frühen 19. Jahrhundert, in C. Zimmermann & H.-P. Ullmann (Eds) *Restaurationssystem und Reformpolitik: Süddeutschland und Preußen im Vergleich*, pp. 225-244. Munich: Oldenbourg.

Educational Data at Late Nineteenth- and Early Twentieth-Century International Expositions: 'accomplished results' and 'instruments and apparatuses'

NOAH W. SOBE

SUMMARY This chapter proposes that the education exhibits at international expositions (or world's fairs) played a significant role in the rise of data in education. Exhibits were carefully executed presentations of a country's education system and examining this history sheds light on many of the tensions and issues that surround the production and circulation of education data today.

Here may be compared the systems of countries many thousands
of miles apart, the systems developed under autocratic and
republican rule, denominational systems with those of the state, all
grouped within a few thousand yards of space, and yet presenting
a clearer illustration of methods, appliances, and results than
could be obtained from an extended tour of the world. (Bancroft,
1893, p. 252)

In his description of the education exhibits at the 1893 World's Columbian Exposition, Robert H. Bancroft, author of the Chicago Fair's official history, lays out a key dimension of producing educational data: the rendering visible and comparable of education processes and practices that otherwise would remain obscured. By bringing the distant and disparate into the same space and onto the same plane of visibility, the international expositions of the late nineteenth and early twentieth centuries generated the matrices of comparative gestures that so powerfully informed the 'reflexive modernization' endeavors of the era. It is widely recognized by scholars that the international expositions of the late nineteenth and early twentieth centuries were important sites where cultural behaviors and expectations were formulated and policed – and also that the expositions played an important role in the development of 'modern' social and institutional structures, inclusive of schooling (Sobe, 2004; Lawn, 2009; Dittrich, 2010, 2013). In this chapter I argue that the education exhibits at international expositions (or world's fairs) played a significant role in the rise of data in education. Examining this history sheds light on many of the tensions and issues that currently surround the production and circulation of education data, particularly the international comparative dimensions of education data.

As is indicated by Bancroft's synopsis, education exhibits at international expositions tended to be very carefully executed presentations of a country's (or a particular unit/sector's) education systems. The exhibits can be usefully understood as a platform for translating information about an education system to external audiences. The quest was to present a 'clear illustration'; and, as I will discuss below, a considerable amount of energy and time was spent to establish what would actually be the best ways to present or demonstrate an education system. In this respect, it is quite appropriate to consider an education exhibit at an exposition to be a form of 'data'. Figure 1 shows an engraving of the Ontario exhibit that was presented at the 1876 Centennial International Exposition in Philadelphia that – with its glass vitrines, model buildings, pictures, wall posters and other artifacts – is representative of many education exhibits.

Figure 1. Engraving of Ontario exhibit at 1876 Centennial International Exposition.

To begin with, what was presented in the several hundred square feet of exhibition hall space was carefully selected. Frequently we can establish a carefully thought-through translation sequence where artifacts and discrete bits of evidence were gathered, distilled or synthesized in some manner and then presented according to particular criteria. The focus of this chapter is on the 'rules' that governed these educational displays.

Almost uniformly, the organizers of the major late nineteenth-/early twentieth-century expositions specified in advance very specific 'research protocols' that were to guide exhibitors in preparing their displays. At the same time, different exhibitors jockeyed with each other – both within a given exposition and across different expositions as they followed one another over the years – to present the most convincing, most reliable and most scientific illustrations of their education systems. These displays played an important role in the early history of the growth of education data and in fact in my conclusion I suggest that there is considerable value to conceptualizing the contemporary production of education data as itself a kind of 'exhibitionary' practice.

The confident and assured 'here may be compared' that Bancroft applied to the 1893 exhibit halls echoes today as the prefatory assumption (implicit or explicit) whenever the results of an international assessment like PISA or TIMSS are published. This also holds for league tables and international rankings, which – the fact they are disputed and debated notwithstanding – also typically operate on the assumption that a reliable space for accurate comparisons can be constructed. The simplification and clarification of the messiness of lived human realities is an enduring aspect of producing data, something we see in Bancroft's assertion that a visit to the Chicago exhibit halls could produce a 'clearer illustration' than 'could be obtained from an extended tour of the world' (1893, p. 252). The clarity of the illustration was particularly valuable because of the general point that a shared, smoothed-out space of visibility affords the identification of differences. In the 1893 exhibit hall this space of visibility was a material and built discursive space. At the Chicago Exposition, Bancroft proposed, education systems could be tracked to different ideological and political positions (authoritarian/republican rule, or different denominational systems). By contrast, the smoothed-out spaces of international comparative visibility of today tend to be, like the OECD spreadsheet, the largely non-physical discursive space of printed pages or PDF files. Quite often these contemporary 'spaces' attract observers because they allow for education systems to be tracked to different organizational and economic arrangements: schools can be compared in terms of their financing, their governance and autonomy but also in relation to national economic wealth and socio-economic equity concerns as well as the (in)famous variable of 'success in the global economy'. The significance of this difference notwithstanding, we see an interesting continuity in that the opening up of a space of visibility and comparison allows for a series of distinctions to be generated and putative 'best practices' to be identified.

Yet, precisely *what* was being displayed and compared remained an unsettled matter at the end of the nineteenth and early twentieth centuries. Bancroft refers to the Chicago education exhibits as illustrating 'methods, appliances, and results' (1893, p. 252). Both at Chicago and at other expositions there was considerable debate on the curatorial and exhibitionary conventions that should specify how a given school system would be presented. One of the key recurring tensions was the question of how one would present data on – what might be referred to in an industrial or economistic idiom as – the 'inputs' and 'outputs' of a given school system. In an official UK report on the Vienna Universal Exhibition of 1873, the British school inspector Reverend James G.C. Fussell opined that 'an educational exhibition is (for the most part at least) an exhibition of appliances and instruments, rather than accomplished results' (1874, p. 239). Yet we find – as is in fact suggested by Fussell's 'for the most part at least' hedging – that across the period under examination here, there were notable oscillations and contestations around the question of whether an education exhibit should feature 'accomplished results' or 'appliances and instruments'. In terms of the former, educators typically turned to student work samples or surveys of educators. What were the appropriate and consequential 'appliances and instruments' to show ran the gamut, as Figure 1 shows to some extent. Exhibits might showcase schoolhouse architecture, design, and ventilation systems; textbooks and other printed matter; globes, maps and other didactic devices; school desks and other items of furniture; as well as maps, charts, graphs, and posters that illustrated various educational aspects such as teacher training, the provisions for centralized and/or local administrative supervision, the geographic distribution of schools, and so forth. Below, with a general but not exclusive focus on US education exhibits, I range across a number of different expositions (from the Vienna exhibition of 1873, through the expositions at Philadelphia 1876, Paris 1889, Chicago 1893, Paris 1900, St Louis 1904, and San Francisco 1915) with the purpose of exploring how the curatorial principles that guided the education exhibits were developed and debated. The 50-year timespan considered here is in part warranted by the extraordinary degree of referentiality from one exposition to the next (Sobe, 2007; Sobe & Rackers, 2009). It was common for nations' 'performances' to be compared with their showings at previous expositions – so much so that exhibit planners themselves were frequently trying to remedy and improve on criticisms levied at the previous expositions. Thus, it makes sense to consider the expositions of this period as an ongoing conversation. We also do find some notable trends and shifts in whether to display 'accomplished results' or 'appliances and instruments'. However, there does not appear to have been a decisive resolution of this question in the period I am examining here.

From a contemporary perspective – as frequently bombarded as we are by the results of international assessments – it is tempting to conclude that in today's day and age this debate has been settled on the side of 'accomplished results'. Administer an identical standardized test to students whether they are under authoritarian or republican rule and regardless of the denomination of their school and we can rather reliably, the thinking goes, ascertain which system produces the best results. This is certainly how PISA and TIMSS results are often discussed.

Yet, as the pilgrimages to Finland of the last decade have demonstrated, educators, researchers, and policymakers must still probe and debate the 'appliances and instruments' that have allegedly led to Finland's apparent success on a recent series of international assessments. This is particularly well illustrated in the United States where the architectural design of Finnish schools has become a particular object of fascination as of late. An exhibit of Finnish school architecture, originally mounted at the Museum of Finnish Architecture in Helsinki in 2011, in 2012 traveled to the United States and was mounted at the Finnish Embassy in Washington, DC, as well as at the American Institute of Architects' Center for Architecture in New York City (Sparks, 2012). Images from this exhibit and the accompanying book (Kasvio, 2011) were used, for example, to illustrate an article by Diane Ravitch (2012) on Finnish education that appeared in the *New York Review of Books* (see Figure 2).

The Kirkkojärvi School in Espoo, Finland, which accommodates about 770 students aged seven to sixteen and also includes a preschool for six-year-olds; from the Museum of Finnish Architecture's exhibition 'The Best School in the World: Seven Finnish Examples from the 21st Century,' which will be on view at the American Institute of Architects' Center for Architecture in New York City this fall

Figure 2. Contemporary Finnish School architecture photograph accompanying 2012 Diane Ravitch article on education in Finland.

The title of Ravitch's article, 'Schools We Can Envy', as well as the alluring and entrancing photographs of the exhibit, uncannily echo the education

45

exhibiting of the late nineteenth- and early twentieth-century international expositions. We can view the Finnish school architecture exhibit as a very deliberate production, dissemination, and consumption of data about schooling. And importantly in this instance, the data has all to do with 'appliances and instruments', i.e. those elements (here, architecture) that help to produce Finland's educational success. Thus, one overarching argument of this chapter is that there is an essential making-things-visible dimension to the production of education data. And, that this includes an interest in attempting to make visible the operational techniques and practices of schooling. Of course, the influence and importance of student test results as the premier education data of our present day and age are undeniable. Yet, this fixation on 'outcomes' is still accompanied by an interest in making visible the workings of school systems that powerfully evokes the vitrines and exhibit halls of the international expositions of the late nineteenth and early twentieth centuries.

Producing Data on the Results and Processes of Education

At the 1876 Centennial Exposition in Philadelphia, one Canadian observer commented that the education exhibits could be characterized as either chiefly consisting of the 'results' of education, or of the 'appliance' of education, or those which combined the two. John George Hodgins, the Deputy Minister of Education for the province of Ontario, noted that Ontario's own exhibit was unique in that it nearly entirely consisted of educational appliances. Other countries, such as Russia, Switzerland, Belgium, and Japan, combined appliances and results in various ways, while the American exhibits focused on results, which Hodgins explained as consisting of 'examples of pupil's work, with large and valuable collections of educational reports and illustrative statistics' (1877, p. 14). This consistency in the exhibitions of various US states was hardly an accident, for during the exposition's planning stages the US Bureau of Education had orchestrated over two years of planning meetings and in November 1875 published a 'Schedule for the Preparation of Students Work for the Centennial Exposition', the first of several circulars issued to provide guidelines for the American exhibitors (Bureau of Education, 1875b).

The major exhibiting US states in 1876 were largely New England and from the Upper Midwest – Massachusetts, New Jersey, Connecticut, Rhode Island, New Hampshire, Illinois, Indiana, Michigan, Iowa – with minor exhibits coming from Maryland, Kentucky, Missouri, Tennessee, Maine, Minnesota, and Wisconsin. At a meeting of state superintendents in Washington, DC at the end of January 1875, John Wickersham of Pennsylvania laid out the stakes for the American exhibits at the coming year's exposition in Philadelphia, which was to be the first international exposition in the United States. He opined that, partly due to the success of the American school house exhibited at the Paris exposition in 1867, foreign visitors would come to the Centennial Exposition with a special interest in US education. An exhibit on US soil would be a severe test, he opined. 'Germany, Austria, Switzerland, France, England, Belgium, and Holland will come, doubtless, prepared to submit their systems of public instruction to a comparison with our own', and Americans 'must be ready to meet them with the best we have' (Bureau of Education, 1875a, p. 57). Wickersham called for the exposition to be a 'full, fair, and systematic representation of American education', and he noted that it would be easy to

> fill our space with the ten thousand articles that may be offered. Material could be had for the asking, I doubt not, sufficient in bulk to fill the whole Exposition-building. A huge mass of miscellaneous articles, with endless repetitions and duplicates even though they could be arranged to look well to the inartistic or unprofessional eye, is not what is wanted. (Bureau of Education, 1875a, p. 59)

Instead, he called for a display that would be 'something of an organism, with its several parts nicely adjusted, if not closely related, to one another' (p. 59). For many countries across the globe, the last three decades of the nineteenth century were a period of intense systemization in the education arena (Müller et al, 1987). In the USA this was also the period when a national education system began to be consolidated, which helps to explain the emphasis on presenting a careful coherent representation of American education.

To accomplish this, the Bureau of Education developed a uniform plan that, among other things, proposed that the US exhibits include student 'examination-manuscripts prepared according to certain prescribed rules' (Bureau of Education, 1875b, p. 8). Few details were left unattended to. The paper used was recommended to be 8 1/4 by 10 1/2 inches in is dimensions; the questions were to be written or printed directly above each answer; each student was to write his or her age, grade, and school name at the head of each manuscript section, and conclude each section with a handwritten statement, 'this accompanying manuscript was written by myself, without aid from any source' (p. 9), followed by a signature. Utmost care was to be taken that the exam questions not be leaked and that only the students who were actually enrolled in the institution took the exams. Though the questions on these work samples were not pre-specified, there was national standardization in that work samples were to be collected between 1 and 15 February, with no more than four hours allowed for students to write on each academic area. According to national planners, in addition to 'properly' displaying American education on an international stage, these efforts would also have domestic benefits in affording 'an opportunity for the public schools of towns and cities and separate institutions of learning of every grade to compare their own work with the work of others, performed under like conditions' (p. 8).

Various state reports on the 1876 Centennial show that these national protocols were widely disseminated and passed along verbatim to districts and to individual schools. This spirit of standardization was also something that states internalized and made their own. Illinois organizers, for example, also provided very specific criteria for the preparation of school models and photographs. Illinois school districts were asked to furnish maps of school grounds in a scale of 200 feet to the inch and building floor plans in a scale of 24 feet to the inch. In taking photographs of school exteriors, Illinois schools were directed that:

> it is important to show enough of the grounds and out-houses to give a correct impression of them. In all cases there should be a collection of pupils in the foreground, so arranged as not to interfere with the view of the building and grounds; pupils to be dressed in every-day attire, and showing all ranks, ages and conditions; some of them being near enough in the foreground to show distinctly their features. (Superintendent of Public Instruction, Illinois, 1877, pp. 386-387)

Additionally, the margin of each photograph was to include information on the cost of the building, the school name, its location (town and county), the building's dimensions, as well as its numbers of students and teachers. Such a level of detail characterizes many of the documents that provided guidance on what and how items should be collected for display at the international expositions. Standardization to allow for comparison within a unified visual field (not 'a huge mass of miscellaneous articles') is a constantly recurring concern in this literature.

The idea of conducting some form of student assessment specifically to produce data that could be exhibited at an international exposition was by no means unique to Philadelphia. In preparing for the 1893 World's Columbian Exposition in Chicago, the New Jersey Department of Public Instruction issued specific instructions and outlined a process that urged individual cities and counties to first mount their own exhibits as a first step towards preparing/selecting items for the state exhibit in Chicago. The New Jersey organizers emphasized the need for the 'honest' work of pupils; provided specifications on time allotments, the paper to be used, that ink was preferable to pencil, and that the bottom right-hand corner of each page was to include the child's name, grade, and age, with the bottom left-hand corner to feature the city/town, school name, and the date. The teacher was to furnish an accompanying statement that made clear the pedagogical purpose (what in a contemporary idiom might be called the 'learning objectives') associated with the students' work samples. The state organizers specified:

> The topic or lesson on which an exhibit is to be made should be one that lends itself readily to such a purpose; it should be typical of the required work of the class or grade, and the result should fairly represent the same. Every exercise should have a separate and distinct end in view from the teacher's stand-point, and the object of the lesson should be made clearly apparent by the pupil's

work. Miscellaneous and objectless work, showing no clearly-defined pedagogical purpose, should have no place in this exhibit. (State Board of Education, New Jersey, 1894, p. 9)

In selecting the work that was to be forwarded to the state to be considered for exhibition in Chicago, New Jersey teachers were directed to choose the *best* work their students produced.

However, when it came to exactly what kind of student work should be prepared for expositions, preferences varied. Across the various expositions, some organizers advocated for work samples not prepared specially for display. The organizers of Kansas' State Normal School exhibit at the 1893 exposition in Chicago agreed at the outset that they would not display 'show work' but rather would show regular student work produced during regular school operations (Board of World's Fair Managers, Kansas, 1894). Student work shown in Michigan's 1893 exhibit, by the organizers' own admission, was 'collected indiscriminately' and then arranged by subject area and grade level in bound volumes that filled two book cases (Weston, 1899, p. 166).

Beyond inter-national and state-to-state comparisons, exposition educational exhibits also allowed for competitive jockeying among different kinds of schools, Catholic education being perhaps the best example of this. The 1893 World's Columbian Exposition in Chicago featured an extensive Catholic education display that primarily featured US schools but also included – in a fascinating if predictable transnational gesture – Catholic schools from archdioceses around the world. The Catholic education exhibit serves as a useful reminder that the international expositions were multidimensional and accomplished different things for different constituencies. Student work samples were a key feature of the Chicago exhibit since they could be held up to silence critics and overcome prejudice against Catholic education. This becomes quite clear from the Catholic exhibit's own official report (Maurelian, 1894), with its extensive reporting on what visitors and commentators had to say. As in the case of New Jersey described above, much of the material in the Catholic exhibit in Chicago appears to have been initially exhibited in the places where it was first gathered. This served local purposes as we see in a statement of the Bishop of Buffalo, NY, who, in discussing an exhibit that was a lead-up to Chicago, claimed, 'the assertion that our Catholic schools are in the slightest degree below the standard of the secular or State schools would not be made by the most prejudiced observer after viewing this exhibition' (Maurelian, 1894, p. 31). Organizers clearly desired that all visitors to Chicago would reach the same conclusion and student work samples had a key role to play. In a report on the exhibit that was published in the journal *Catholic World* (and in a quintessential example of the phenomenal inter-textual referentiality/'house of mirrors effect' [Sobe & Ortegón, 2009] that accompanied the expositions), John O'Shea quoted the secular German-language Chicago newspaper *Staats Zeitung* as reporting that 'those defective patterns of humanity who are running our public schools' could only exhibit

models of buildings, or their photographs, methods and means
bought by the state at a heavy expense, but not the results of the
schools, not the proofs of education ... The weakness of the public
schools shows all the more forcibly the strength of the Catholic
educational institutions at the Expositions. Instead of beautiful
building models and costly methods, they have exhibited the
practical results of their schools. (O'Shea, 1893, p. 189)

While, as Figure 1 showed above, many exposition education exhibits were
tightly packed with all manner of objects, photographs of the Catholic
education exhibits in Chicago show a particular density of student work
displays. In this instance, presenting the 'results' of education served a
particular set of interests, especially as Catholic schools in the late nineteenth
century sometimes faced the charge of being less well funded and equipped
than public schools.

Across the period treated here, interest in presenting educational
outcomes waxed and waned. The Panama-Pacific International Exposition
held in San Francisco in 1915 is an interesting case. The chief organizer of
the education exhibit hall, Alvin E. Pope, noted in an organizing document,
'we have outgrown the old-style educational display, consisting of
comprehensive, duplicate exhibits, composed chiefly of pupils' work' (as
quoted in Ryan, 1916, p. 7). Frank Morton Todd, the author of the official
history of the San Francisco Exposition, wrote:

The world had outgrown the old-style display of pupil's papers
showing how much like the copy book little Johnny and little Mary
could write, and what long words they could spell at the age of
seven years without getting blots on the paper; for, people were
beginning to see that the best spellers did not always turn out to
be the best sellers. Moreover, with hard enough drill on the
teacher's part it sometimes happened that a blotless prodigy in a
most inferior school surpassed the best product of the good
institutions. Such exhibits showed nothing valuable, and the
public had found it out. (Todd, 1921, pp. 36-37)

In place of student work samples (however produced) the San Francisco
organizers invited both American states and foreign countries to highlight
those educational activities that they excelled in. In the case of the US
exhibits, 'invitations were restricted in order to avoid duplication and the
special exhibits were so assembled as to portray the salient features of
modern American education' (Todd, 1921, p. 37). The central organizing
principle of the exhibits of the American states was that each participating
state would confine its exhibit to 'one distinct system or process in which he
excelled; to one definite lesson which he was capable of teaching the world'.
The objective, stated in terms very similar to those used by Wickersham in
1875, was that by having each state select systems or processes in which they
excelled, the exhibits of all the states together would add up to a cohesive

display. And in the end, as claimed in the US Bureau of Education's official report, this goal for a 'unified display rather than numerous exhibits' was 'carried out consistently' (Ryan, 1916, p. 6).

In other publications (Sobe, 2004, 2007) I have argued that the recurring juxtaposition of 'numerous exhibits' with a 'unified display' suggests an interest in constructing a coherent visual (and intellectual) field and accords with other features of the San Francisco exposition. A similar discourse emerges with regard to the exposition's architecture and color scheme, all of which betray a preoccupation with new awareness of the manipulability of human perception and the desire to direct this manipulability toward progress and advancement. In the 'new-style' displays in San Francisco's education palace, exhibitors were to present something in which they excelled. In response, to offer several examples, Massachusetts decided to focus its exhibit on vocational secondary education and textile education; New York chose to emphasize the 'centralization of authority' that marked its school system; and, California put forward its school architecture and the use of 'educational motion pictures' as the state's strongest educational features (Egilbert, 1915; Massachusetts Board of Panama-Pacific Managers, 1915; New York State Panama-Pacific Exposition Commission, 1916). In short, 1915 witnessed a shift towards 'appliances' or 'instruments' as opposed to 'results' and 'outcomes'. At the same time, the example of the 1915 exposition in San Francisco is a useful reminder not to impose a historical narrative that emphasizes the gradual uni-directional consolidation and inevitable rise to the top of one particular mechanism for producing educational data or another.

Before concluding this brief and episodic review of the curatorial and exhibitionary principles that structured education exhibits at international expositions, it is worth examining two additional mechanisms that were relied upon to produce education data and render visible the workings of schooling. First is the teacher survey, that, at the time, appears to have fitted with relative comfort alongside student work as an acceptable window into student learning. A good example of this is the research study conducted on US kindergarten education in preparation for the 1900 exposition in Paris. In a report written for the official catalogue of the US exhibit, Susan Blow (1900) described a study conducted on Blow's behalf by Laura Fisher, the director of Boston's 69 kindergartens. To attempt to ascertain the results of kindergarten education, all first-grade teachers in Boston were asked to write about whether the children in their classrooms who had attended kindergarten differed from, or advanced more quickly, than those first graders who hadn't attended kindergarten. The researcher received 163 responses and from the report we learn that she went to great lengths to ensure the reliability and validity of her data. From the initial set of responses, 36 letters were eliminated because fewer than 10% of the respondents' first-grade students had attended kindergarten (or attended kindergarten for more than several weeks). Then, of the remaining 127 letters, 25 were deemed unfavorable while 102 were determined to show the positive effects of the kindergarten experience. Fisher's research protocols and procedures bear resemblance to the preceding descriptions of the conventions that were to govern the production of student work samples. And they similarly represent an effort to furnish data that can be used to effect comparisons.

The second additional way that schooling was rendered visible at late nineteenth- and early twentieth-century international expositions was through efforts to present evidence of change in individual students over time. In a circular published in advance of the 1893 World's Columbian Exposition, the chief organizer of the US Bureau of Education exhibit at Chicago, C. Wellman Parks, recommended that 'if possible, some of the earlier work of the same pupils should be shown' (State Board of Education, New Jersey, 1894, p. 9), though it is not clear that many US states followed his advice. However, at Chicago, France – seemingly of its own accord – did present a longitudinal exhibit showing photographs and work samples of a single student who was profiled across his entire elementary and secondary education career (Dittrich, 2010). Nonetheless, the most common way to show student progress and achievement was through the exhibition of actual students and live classrooms.

'Live' educational demonstrations at international expositions took many forms with demonstration kindergarten classrooms probably being the most significant and most often-recurring form. Maria Montessori's methods received a notable launching in the USA when she herself attended and led a demonstration kindergarten at the Panama-Pacific International Exposition in San Francisco in 1915 (see Sobe, 2004, for an extensive discussion). As much as they attempted to showcase progress and modernity, international expositions also – and relatedly – frequently played an unsavory role in exoticizing so-called 'primitive' peoples. Alongside kindergartens the second major form of live demonstrations was displays of non-White, non-Europeans receiving Western educations. At Philadelphia in 1876 the State of Connecticut featured 115 Chinese students who were studying at a variety of institutions in the state. The group appear to have been brought to Philadelphia mostly as exhibition attendees and they were not set up in a 'human zoo' demonstration classroom. Yet in some important ways they seem to have been considered part of the Connecticut display. Francis Walker's (1880) official report on the awards issued across the Centennial Exhibition devotes over 300 pages to describing the education exhibits and remarks of Connecticut:

> The body of one hundred and fifteen Chinese students escorted to
> the Exhibition by the honorable Secretary of the State Board of
> Education afforded the Judges an unexpected and highly enjoyed
> opportunity to witness, in their persons, the quickness of mind
> and adaptability to new circumstances and conditions, as well as
> the admirable development, which characterize them and have

already given them a very honorable rank among the best pupils of our best New England schools. (Walker, 1880, p. 22)

Perhaps the most significant spectacle of non-Westerners proving their capacity for Western learning occurred at the 1904 St Louis Exposition within the vast ethnological exhibit that the USA set up in order to introduce its new colonial possession (acquired from Spain after 1898) to the American – and a world – public. Approximately 1200 Filipinos and Filipinas were brought to Missouri and organized into villages that were to represent different stages of 'civilizational' evolution. A model missionary school was displayed where loin-clothed Igorots (one of the purportedly 'higher-ranked' ethnic groups) demonstrated their potential to be further civilized by singing 'My Country 'Tis of Thee' to President Roosevelt on his visit to the exposition. Live bodies thus offered one of the additional means for providing evidence about the validity and successfulness of education.

Conclusion

In this chapter I have argued that the expositions of the late nineteenth and early twentieth centuries played an important role in the rise of data in education. They played a role in the development and professionalization of educational research that still warrants considerable additional research. Above I have paid scant attention to the statistical data that was presented at expositions. More research is needed on the way that the expositions and the various statistical congresses held concurrently to them shaped national and subnational data-gathering practices. Yet, it is clear from the above that, in gathering student work samples, photographs, architectural models, textbooks, and occasionally living demonstration-students in one place, 'within a few thousand yards of space', the expositions served as powerful centers of calculability.

Exhibitors and attendees alike were well aware of the matrices of comparative gazes that accompanied the making-visible of education processes and policies. The expositions can be considered a 'global scopic system' (Knorr-Cetina, 2008; Sobe & Ortegón, 2009; Sobe, 2013) that, like a prism, focused light and attention on a very carefully smoothed-out space of visibility. Just as in many contemporary accountability systems, there were any number of observers/participants who increasingly paid attention to the reflected or represented reality over embodied, pre-reflective experience and knowledge.

As Martin Lawn notes in the introduction to this volume, within the past few years quantitative data has gained enormous influence in education systems around the globe. We have seen education data moving beyond the purview of the specialists and expert groups that often produce it, to filter into the public representations and perceptions of education systems. As Lawn puts it, 'the visualisation of the data ... has changed over time, especially in its movement from an expert to a public act' (p. 8). However, this point, while certainly true, speaks to the value of examining the era of the nineteenth-century international expositions, where we see a similar intermingling between the use of education data by expert and lay populations.

The design and coordination of the exposition exhibits themselves was the responsibility of educational specialists, yet there was an intriguing ambiguity in ways that planners sought to appeal both to their peers and to the general public(s) who would attend the events. It is important then that the expositions were not just specialized scholarly or professional events but were public events where different countries' education systems were laid open to general scrutiny and evaluation – with the concurrent possibility of scandalization accompanying a 'poor showing' and national pride and becoming a destination for foreign study tours following for the most successful performers. In this respect, among others, one can say that the late nineteenth- and early twentieth-century expositions reflected some of the same dynamics and tensions that, for example, accompany the OECD PISA tests of today. And, the expositions remind us that the 'accomplished results' of schools continue to interlace with the ways that we make visible education's 'instruments and apparatuses'.

References

Bancroft, Hubert H. (1893) *The Book of the Fair: an historical and descriptive presentation*. Chicago: Bancroft.

Blow, Susan (1900) Kindergarten Education, in Nicholas M. Butler (Ed.) *Education in the United States*. Albany: J.B. Lyon.

Board of World's Fair Managers, Kansas (1894) *Report of the Kansas Board of World's Fair Managers*. Topeka: Hamilton Printing Company.

Bureau of Education, US (1875a) *Proceedings of the Department of Superintendence of the National Educational Association at Washington, DC, January 27 and 28, 1875, Circular No. 1*. Washington, DC: Government Printing Office.

Bureau of Education, US (1875b) *Schedule for the Preparation of Students' Work for the Centennial Exposition, Circular No. 8*. Washington, DC: Government Printing Office.

Dittrich, Klaus (2010) Experts Going Transnational: education at world exhibitions during the second half of the nineteenth century. PhD thesis, University of Portsmouth. http://eprints.port.ac.uk/1676/

Dittrich, Klaus (2013) Appropriation, Representation and Cooperation as Transnational Practices: the example of Ferdinand Buisson, in Isabella Löhr & Ronald Wenzlhuemer (Eds) *The Nation State and Beyond: governing globalization processes in the nineteenth and early twentieth centuries*, pp. 149-176. Berlin: Springer-Verlag.

Egilbert, W.D. (1915) California's Education Exhibit – the Panama-Pacific International Exposition, in California Teachers' Association (Ed.) *Complimentary Souvenir Book: Fifty-Third Annual Convention National Education*

Association and International Congress of Education. San Francisco: Arthur Henry Chamberlain.

Fussell, James George C. (1874) Educational Appliances, in Great Britain Royal Commission for the Vienna Universal Exhibition in 1873 (Ed.) *Reports of the Vienna Universal Exhibition*, vol. 3, pp. 236-289. London: Eyre & Spottiswoode.

Hodgins, J. George (1877) *Special Report to the Honorable Minister of Education on the Ontario Educational Exhibit and the Educational Features of the International Exhibition at Philadelphia, 1876.* Toronto: Hunter and Rose.

Kasvio, Maija (Ed.) (2011) *The Best School in the World: seven Finnish examples from the 21st century.* Helsinki: Art-Print Oy.

Knorr Cetina, K. (2008) Microglobalization, in I. Rossi (Ed.), *Frontiers of Globalization Research: theoretical and methodological approaches*, pp. 65-92. New York: Springer.

Lawn, Martin (2009) *Modelling the Future: exhibitions and the materiality of education.* Oxford: Symposium Books.

Massachusetts Board of Panama-Pacific Managers (1916) *Massachusetts at the Panama-Pacific International Exposition, San Francisco, California, 1915. Report of the Board of Panama-Pacific Managers for Massachusetts.* Boston: Wright & Potter Printing Company, State Printers.

Maurelian, Brother (1894) Final Report: Catholic Educational Exhibit, World's Columbian Exposition. Chicago: (World's Fair).

Muller, Detlef, Ringer, Fritz & Simon, Brian (1987) *The Rise of the Modern Education System.* Cambridge: Cambridge University Press.

New York State Panama-Pacific Exposition Commission (1916) *State of New York at the Panama Pacific International Exposition.* Albany: J.B. Lyon Company.

O'Shea, John J. (1893) Catholic Education at the World's Fair, *Catholic World*, 58(344), 186-203.

Ravitch, Diane (2012) Schools We Can Envy, *New York Review of Books*, 8 March, pp. 19-20.

Ryan, W. Carson (1916) Education Exhibits at the Panama-Pacific International Exposition, *Bureau of Education Bulletin*, no. 1.

Sobe, Noah W. (2004) Challenging the Gaze: the subject of attention and a 1915 Montessori demonstration classroom, *Educational Theory*, 54(3), 281-297.

Sobe, Noah W. (2007) Attention and Spectatorship: educational exhibits at the Panama-Pacific International Exposition, San Francisco 1915, in Volker Barth (Ed.) *Innovation and Education at International Expositions*, pp. 95-116. Paris: International Bureau of Expositions.

Sobe, Noah W. (2013) Teacher Professionalization and the Globalization of Schooling, in Terri Seddon & John S. Levin (Eds) *Educators, Professionalism and Politics: global transitions, national spaces and professional projects (World Yearbook of Education, 2013)*, pp. 42-54. London: Routledge.

Sobe, Noah W. & Ortegón, Nicole (2009) Scopic Systems, Pipes, Models and Transfers in the Global Circulation of Educational Knowledge and Practices, in T. Popkewitz & F. Rizvi (Eds) *Globalization and the Study of Education*, pp. 49-66. New York: NSSE/Teachers College Press.

Sobe, Noah W. & Rackers, Carrie (2009) Fashioning Writing Machines: typewriting and handwriting exhibits at US World's Fairs 1893-1915, in Martin Lawn (Ed.) *Modelling the Future Exhibitions and the Materiality of Education*, pp. 87-105. Oxford: Symposium Books.

Sparks, Sarah D. (2012) Form + Function = Finnish Schools, *Education Week*, 18 July, p. 9.

State Board of Education, New Jersey (1894) *Catalogue and Report of Special Committee of the New Jersey School Exhibit at the World's Columbian Exposition at Chicago, 1893*. Trenton, NJ: John L. Murphy Pub.

Superintendent of Public Instruction, Illinois (1877) *Eleventh Biennial Report*. Springfield: D.W. Lusk.

Todd, Frank Morton (1921) *The Story of the Exposition*, vol. IV. New York: G.P. Putnam's Sons.

Walker, Frances A. (1880) *International Exhibition 1876 – reports and awards*, vol. VIII. Washington, DC: Government Printing Office.

Weston, Isaac Mellen (1899) *Report of the Board of World's Fair Managers for the State of Michigan*. Lansing: Robert Smith.

(Mis-)Trust in Numbers:[1] shape shifting and directions in the modern history of data in Swedish educational reform

JOAKIM LANDAHL & CHRISTIAN LUNDAHL

SUMMARY In this chapter the authors explore the uses and meanings of data in Swedish educational reform, practice and discourse from roughly the 1940s up to the present day. Their survey covers both national data and international data and includes quantitative as well as qualitative data. They start in the 1940s with two empirical examples that in a way show an antithetical attitude towards data. Travel accounts from America were based on a qualitative approach, and expressed the attitude that the schools studied were important because they were different, modern and inspiring. At roughly the same time, standardised testing was introduced as a technique of connecting the different parts of the school system and rationalising student admission processes. The consequences of this standardisation came under severe attack during the late 1960s and 1970s, resulting eventually in the introduction of a criterion-referenced grading system. Finally, the authors highlight the fact that the last few decades have seen the flourishing of such things as international assessment and school inspection, and there has been an increased emphasis on grades and testing. These examples illustrate that the meanings and techniques of data are objects of a continuous negotiation where sometimes even resistance towards measuring tends to be based on measurements.

Introduction

Over time we see that an educational system uses various kinds of data to describe, to understand or to control itself. In the production and/or the use of educational data, different actors use different technologies of looking at and investigating educational matters. If, by 'data', we simply mean information about something or someone we can see that the history of data in Swedish education is very long and has many forms and shapes. Data

57

changes in relation to purposes of use, in relation to who produces it and how it can be produced, and of course in relation to its consequences. Data thus can take many shapes and forms, and it can be used for many different purposes. In this chapter we describe the various shapes and forms of educational data that have played an important role in shaping Swedish education, from the 1940s to the present. The chosen time period is strongly associated with the comprehensive school reform that gained momentum in the 1940s, when governmental reports laid the foundation for a new school system that gradually came into existence and was finally realised as nine-year compulsory schooling in 1962. This reform actually consisted of many small reforms and changes that occurred in two major phases – first we have the preparation and starting-up phase between the 1880s and the 1960s, and then we have the restructuring and replacement phase from the 1980s until the present day. By looking at how data was used in the construction of the comprehensive school and how data was discussed in media such as teacher journals, teacher training materials and even student union materials, we can illustrate major traits, changes and directions both in data production and in its usage and consequences. Of course, how data is shaped varies greatly in relation to what it is about. In this text we mainly look at data about learning and learning outcomes.

In order to extract data, someone or something has to be made visible. For something to be visible, there must be someone who watches. Of course, it is possible to hide from someone who is trying to see you, or keep secrets when asked questions. But when the eye meets a target, description becomes possible. Descriptions of an object must be visualised in some way in order to become data. Now the question arises, is this description valid and reliable, and for whom, and under what conditions?

Data production can to a high degree be seen as a negotiation over validity and reliability between different actors in the educational field. We have here a kind of eternal conflict between what Zygmunt Bauman has described as the culture of gamekeepers and that of gardeners, that is, between a pre-modern and modern way of organising societal reproduction (1989). The gamekeeper represents one view of reproduction, and the gardener another one. The gamekeeper lets culture reproduce itself from generation to generation without a conscious design, while the gardener does not rely on culture to reproduce itself. Gardeners impose order. Gardeners and gamekeepers were metaphors actually used to describe different views of reproduction during the eighteenth century, but we find similar positions in dichotomies like positivism versus hermeneutics, quantitative data versus qualitative data, or in educational concepts such as formative versus summative classroom assessments. No matter what terminology we use to describe these differences, it seems that tensions and dynamics in an educational system are created by: 1. the method of collecting of data; 2. the standardisation of data; 3. the use of data. Using data in educational change entails a constant deliberation over validity claims – an act of calibration. As

Danziger writes: in the end, behind every score there is a judgement, a judgement that this or that is a measure of, for example, intelligence, talent, or school result (Danziger, 1997, p. 83). Judgements are often debatable in terms of validity – do these data really represent X, do we dare to make a decision based upon what we know about X, when we measure X do we risk making it even worse for X, and so on. These debates of course look different if they come up in relation to data in the form of statistics or in the shape of photography.

Data is about making the school visible, and might therefore be seen as a panoptical power. However, in order to make sense of the way in which data operates, we will argue that there are some limitations to the concept of panopticon (cf. Alford, 2000; Boyne, 2000; Haggerty, 2006; Otter, 2008; Gallagher, 2010). One way of getting a more complex picture is by referring to the opposite phenomenon: synoptical power. The concept was introduced by Mathiesen (1997), who used it to describe the phenomenon that many watch the few, exemplified by modern television. This concept can also be applied to data in education. Data is not just something that visualises the people; it is also visible in itself, and ultimately it makes the people in political power visible. We suggest that synoptical power is important for understanding resistance as well as obedience towards the use of data in education, and therefore it increases our understanding of how data changes. On this point we disagree with Mathiesen, who argued that synopticism results in an augmentation of the existing power structures. As pointed out by Doyle (2011), this is a one-sided view: synoptical power is also vulnerable, and subject to criticism.

Representing International School Systems with Photographs (1940s)

The way that data operates as a way of making international comparisons underwent a sea change during the twentieth century. The quantitative data that circulates today, mainly under the flag of PISA, represents a dramatic deviation towards the ways that data used to be collected about foreign school systems. Time-consuming practices such as letter writing, travel accounts, world exhibitions, international journals and teacher meetings provided dominant ways of gaining knowledge about schools in other countries. We will shortly describe one of these data types, the travel account, and will discuss the case of the American school in the 1940s. Discussing how this model country was represented, we will particularly focus on the role of photography in disseminating ideas of what a good school might be.

Although schooling is a national enterprise, it has always been influenced by teaching methods and school organisation in other countries. This also means that the quality of the Swedish school system has been compared with other national school systems, a comparison that has often led to the conclusion that some ideas from abroad were superior. Still, this comparison was not to any significant extent based on quantitative data. By reading travel accounts from this era, it becomes possible to discuss what kind of knowledge was produced about other countries before the advent of quantitative data in international comparisons.

We will take the American school system as a case in point, focusing on four travel accounts from the 1940s: *In American Schools* (Hermansson, 1940), *Democratic Education in the USA* (Skäringer-Larsson, 1941), *Contact with America* (Myrdal & Myrdal, 1941) and *Social Education in American Schools* (Casserberg, 1948). In the 1940s, the American school very much occupied the same position in the world of teaching as Finland does today. The American school was looked upon with great curiosity, and was seen as a role model, it was the educational utopia of its time. However, the descriptions of the American school differed in many ways from how Finland is being described today, in respect of both how data was collected and what kind of message the data was said to convey.

The travel accounts from America were produced at a time when statistical comparisons between national school systems were non-existent. The American school did not top any list, yet it was considered worth studying. In fact, although there was no list that 'objectively' identified the American school as 'best', the reader gets the impression that this was indeed the best type of school. Now, what quality of the American school system was it that was so irresistible to emulate? In short, it was certain values: modernity, democracy and pupil orientation.

What stands out in the travel accounts from America is the richness of detail. It is obvious that the authors really tried to understand the practical reality of schooling. They write about the different school subjects, and do not limit themselves to discussing just reading, writing and arithmetic. They also write about architecture, school books and teaching methods. They describe the content of schooling, what is learnt but also how it is learnt, that is, the teaching methods used. Rather than giving abstract descriptions of the American school system, they convey highly concrete details about learning and instruction inside and outside of the classrooms.

This richness of detail corresponds to an appraisal of what characterises the good school: its versatility. While it was argued that American schools were indeed performing well even in a traditional sense, the fundamental strength of the American progressive schools was that they taught so much more than traditional schools of the time did.

One particular method of collecting data from America – the use of photographs – illuminates the attitude towards what kind of knowledge it was possible to gather about a foreign country. The photographs provided concrete information about a great variety of phenomena, and did not portray teaching only in a limited sense, but also showed the wider pedagogical environment. This might for example include contact with parents, the library, the school patrol, the playground and the school cafeteria. Everything seems to have been interesting for the photographer. Not only is the library depicted, but also the 'excellent card system' used to categorise the books, and also the fact that at one school the library is taken care of by pupils in the fifth grade (Figure 1). Not only were teachers and pupils depicted, but also parents visiting schools, e.g. for a 'mothers tea'.

»Det fanns utmärkta kortsystem av olika slag.»   *Lincoln school, New York.*

Figure 1. The photographs of American schools depicted pupils actively searching for knowledge in a variety of ways. This is a picture of the card system used in the library. Source: Ester Hermansson, *In American Schools* 1940.

This richness in details must be partly related to the specific features of photography as a medium. As Susan Sontag pointed out in her seminal essay *On Photography*, the introduction of photography established a new visual code characterised by its insatiability. 'In teaching us a new visual code, photographs alter and enlarge our notions of what is worth looking at and what we have a right to observe. They are a grammar and, even more importantly, an ethics of seeing' (Sontag, 2001, p. 3). This might sound like technological determinism, and perhaps it is, but our point here is that the photographs in the travel accounts harmonised with, and probably amplified, an attitude towards reality that was already there, namely that nearly everything was of interest.

The use of photographs was also a way of making the American school visible, and therefore real. Sontag again: 'Photographs furnish evidence. Something heard about, but doubt, seems proven when we're shown a photograph of it' (2001, p. 5). While Sontag emphasises photography as a nostalgic medium, a technique that visualises the past, we see the opposite in the travel accounts from American schools. To a great extent the photographs seem to depict modernity itself. By depicting modern education, it became possible to imagine a more modern school. The modern school was not just a vision fixed on paper, it was not a utopia. The pictures spoke for themselves: the modern, child-oriented school existed. It was a perfectly feasible and reasonable creation, and it was expressed in multiple ways.

The comparisons between Sweden and the United States were based on the premise that there was no clear scale for comparison. The absence of standardised, quantitative measures for pupil performance drew attention to other aspects of schooling than what appear in today's international comparisons. This created a wider appreciation of what constituted a good school, and made the idea of measuring performance in a simple way irrelevant. This is evident, for example, when Myrdal and Myrdal (1941) discuss the question of whether American pupils actually learn anything in schools. Comparing the American pupil with the European pupil, they say that the former is actually outdone by the latter when it comes to performance in the final exams. However, they continue, a few years after the final exam, the American pupils will have retained a lot more knowledge.

The American travel accounts were, in other words, rich in qualitative data and poor in quantitative data. This does not mean that they actively resisted the idea of measuring another school system with data, but rather that statistics were not relevant for describing what was seen, heard, read or experienced in other ways when abroad in the 1940s. However, as we now will see, a totally different picture is given if we turn our attention towards the national educational system in Sweden at the very same time period.

Establishing a National School System by Using Standardised Data (1940s-1960s)

Photography could play an important role in providing the educational system with external reflections motivating a new educational system, but in building a new comprehensive school system there was a need for a more standardised language that could unite the different parts and agents of Swedish education. Quantitative data is probably more effective in building national systems than photographs.

Using Data to Calibrate School Reform

During the 1880s in Sweden a movement was born claiming that the primary school should be the basis of a unified, comprehensive, school system. It took until the late 1920s before this idea really started to affect the organisation of Swedish education, and until 1962 for its full completion to be realised. During this process, data, and especially standardised data about students and their abilities, played a very important role both in the practical realisation of the comprehensive school and in its symbolical legitimisation.

There is a difference between just classifying and mapping, and actually organising, a group, actions or even societies from social classification. For the latter to be technically and symbolically possible there is a need for calibration. The new modern methods, especially those connected with the science of psychology and pedagogy, had far greater impact, not least because of how their proponents managed to calibrate validity claims with political concepts and reforms.

In his analysis of the language of psychology, Kurt Danziger writes that '[s]trictly speaking, there are no "raw" data in science. Whatever forms the subject of scientifically informed perception is already classified in some way' (Danziger, 1997, p. 189). As in England, Germany and France for example, Sweden also started to use standardised measurements in order to organise students with special needs in asylums or in special classes in the early twentieth century. This kind of organisation already existed, but in this way categories of institutional practice were connected to psychological categories and standardised techniques of investigation. In the first decades of the twentieth century, most test development was about individual testing but, as the ability to construct group tests developed, more and more children could be tested for more purposes (Ydesen et al, 2013). In contrast to most other countries in Europe during the mid-twentieth century, Sweden introduced large-scale standardised testing, which in Sweden was called *Standardprov*, in order to make the teachers' grading of their students more objective. Standardised testing was seen as a prerequisite in a norm-referenced grading system where children's achievements were supposed to be compared with each other.[2] The aim was to replace the admission test at the grammar school with the simpler and faster procedure of using the final grades from primary school for selection to the grammar school (Lundahl, 2009; Lundahl & Waldow, 2009). Before standardised grades were used, teachers had to prepare the pupils who wanted to go to grammar school with the consequence that the elementary school had to give the rest of the students an education that was far too advanced. More than 75% of the student population in 1950 did not go to grammar school (SCB, 1974). In order to preserve the elementary teachers' right to teach at a more basic level, grades were seen as a possible substitute for the old admission test on classical subjects. The grammar teachers did not like this idea so it had to be legitimised, and so it was with the help of standardised testing. By standardising the grades with help from external testing, it also became possible to accept the primary school as the foundation of the educational system. Sweden had a tracked school system with parallel classes in years 4 to 6. Between 1949 and 1962 all the school districts in Sweden changed that into a unified school system, seeing standardised grading as a prerequisite for the system to hold together. Standardised data became the means and content of the communication between the different practices and actors in the system. And it did so in a quick and seemingly rational way (Lundahl & Waldow, 2009).

Another important prerequisite for the establishment of the comprehensive school was to find reasonable educational standards. In order to decide the normal ability of a school child at a certain age, the so-called 'school readiness test' (*skolmognadsprov*) was developed (Hägglund, 1990). The data produced from that test was used in two ways. First, it was used to calibrate the curriculum to create a level of a difficulty suitable for the 'normal child'. The second usage of this data was in relation to the decision on the length of the primary school period, or in other words when the tracking should start (at ages 11-12 or at ages 13-14).

Many of the ideas behind the standardised test came from America. The Swedish test developers were, as in the States, trained during the Second World War to construct and carry out group tests. After the war, many of the psychometricians that had been working at the so-called Institute of Military Psychology with group testing moved over to the field of education. The ongoing school reform provided standardised testing with an ideal playground perfectly suited for correlations and deviations. The new field offered this psychological brand of educational science a shelter for its own development. Not being very coherent in theory, skills in methodology gave this brand scientific status (cf. Danziger, 1990; Porter, 1995). Abstract and numerical calculations functioned as a way to gain legitimacy (Figure 2).

The whole procedure of student admission could now be conceptualised as an objective matter. The teachers of course did not really like this. Their judgement had been replaced. But, as Porter (1995) writes about the similar development in the USA, the teachers were mostly unmarried women and did not really have the professional self-confidence to put up against these 'men of standardisation'. And of course, they might have been persuaded to accept standardised testing when they read in teacher journals things like this: 'The standards of the test are calculated in compliance with the national grading regulations. When standardised tests are used, grades may therefore be automatically distributed in different levels according to the rules' (*Svensk skoltidning*, 1963, p. 20). What can be more objective than automatically distributed grades?

Figure 2. The statistical analysis concerning the distribution of grades based on the scores at the standardized test. Illustration by Yngve Svalander, in Husén et al, 1956, p. 28.

Calibrating Data Production as in Relation to Recipients

During this time, there was little evidence of the consequences of measurement and standardisation. The government and the researchers did not calibrate their claims with consequences but rather with hopes and dreams. Standardised measurements became associated with the goods to come – a fair distribution of life chances (Figure 3), without anyone really reflecting about possible backwash effects (Lundahl, 2006).

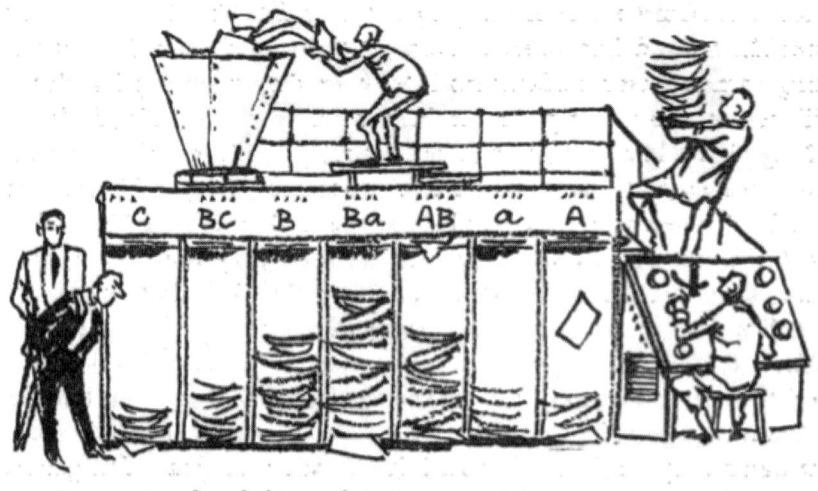

Proven ger så småningom betyg.

Figure 3. The actual distribution of grades based on test scores.
Illustration by Yngve Svalander in Husén et al, 1956, p. 33.

The major political argument behind the comprehensive school reform had been to increase the equality in the educational system. Mostly framed as equality of opportunity (Hadenius, 1990), the combination of high stakes and an easy measurable ideal outcome propelled standardised measurement towards general mistrust. It became easy for the ones who wanted to criticise the government to use the data that the government had produced in order to achieve their goals, against the government. Data revealed that even if there now was equality of opportunity, a huge inequality in results had been exposed (e.g. Callewaert & Lundgren, 1976). Schooling did not function as an equalising factor but rather the other way around: it was seen to manifest social reproduction. Even more interestingly, much of the blame for the social reproduction was put on the equalising instruments of grading and standardised testing. This led to a campaign of resistance against these technologies, which contributed to some major changes in the production of data (which we have a closer look at below).

When we look at the period between the 1930s and the late 1960s, it is obvious that it is not enough to think of testing as a panoptical power. In the history of testing and of quantification it seems that people in general have been quite sceptical towards social classification (cf. Gould, 1981). Claiming validity is actually a vulnerable business – as a scholar, for example, you expose yourself to criticism from peers but also from the test-taker and/or public opinion about your results. Quantification is not, as Barry Barnes (in Porter, 1995, p. 98) put it: power plus legitimacy, but power minus discretion. Every data-collecting authority exposes itself to the potential synoptical counter-power of the masses. In order to get acceptance for data, and especially the interpretation of data, the measurements need to be validated in relation to other judgements. Claiming that a national standardised test makes grading automatic and objective, or, for example, using optimistically illustrated pictures (see Figures 2 and 3), can be seen as ways of handling, or forestalling, criticism. At the same time, the idea of a national test measuring the intelligence of the pupils moved the responsibility for school achievements from the teacher to the child (cf. Madaus & O'Dwyer, 1999). The idea was from the beginning partly adapted to teacher culture.

Restructuring the School System by Criticising Standardised Data (1968-1989)

Resistance against data in education is not new [3] but it changes form and reasons throughout history. The resistance in the 1970s was very much related to the hopes and promises of the data collection in the investigations into the comprehensive school and of the standardised testing and grading system.

Teacher Resistance

If we consider the leading critical left-wing teacher journal *KRUT* (Journal for Educational Criticism),[4] between 1977 and 1987, we find some interesting coincidences that help explain a little further how resistance can be born and how it contributes to the calibration of data and data interpretation in an educational discourse. The journal *KRUT* was a progressive and left-wing-oriented journal for teachers and other school staff. *KRUT* is an example of the development of a heterodox position within the field of data production. It represents the birth of a new discursive centre and the possibility of taking a dialectical position in the production of data using knowledge assessments (cf. Lundahl, 2006). The criticism that was expressed in *KRUT* and in similar communities started to grow out of a reading of reports of governmental commissions. The reports, and their suggestions, were many, and the different authors in *KRUT* wrote that they had difficulty understanding all of the intentions of the government. The governing of the school was seen as weak, manipulative and rigid. In line with this 'suspiciousness', several articles were published stating that the school had a 'hidden curriculum', which is an interesting paradox in relation to the fact that educational results were more overt than ever before. The government and the National Board of Education claimed that the Swedish comprehensive school was 'a school for all', but the articles in *KRUT* tried to show how the comprehensive school actually reproduced the social structure of the capitalist system. The authors relied, among other things, on the statistics produced by the system they were criticising and thus, so to speak, used synoptical counter-power to visualise the people in political power. This kind of criticism was informed by sociological theories, especially those of Marx and Bourdieu. It was important for the editors of *KRUT* to show what function school 'actually' had in society. In parallel to this discussion, several articles were published dealing with the effect of external testing on teaching in schools. External tests were seen as a threat to the teachers' autonomy concerning their teaching. Both the social reproductive function of assessment and the perceived threat to teacher autonomy provided a motive to fight against assessment in education. The journal was in itself part of that fight and published articles about the 'street-level' struggle teachers and students had started in the schools. Several strategies were applied to encourage 'the fight'. One example is the use of pictures that commented and made jokes about the opponents (Figure 4).

Figure 4. The boycotting of standardized test. A student and a teacher
movement. Postcard published in KRUT, 1983, no. 27/28, p. 67.

To some degree, it is possible to say that the struggle against various kinds of assessments led to a changed reality. More importantly, it can be seen as an example of how the discourse of data production was provided with an awareness of some of its negative aspects, although, as Lundahl (2006) noted, this awareness was delivered without any *pedagogical* alternatives concerning assessments and other forms of data production. When assessment criticism was well established, it relied on existing data, existing structures to produce data, and formal concepts and terms to talk about and describe assessments in education. In that way the critics were prisoners of the standardisation discourse described earlier. At the same time, theoretical concepts and models were imported from other fields of knowledge to interpret the 'new' information on assessment consequences mainly focusing on 'the bigger picture'. This indicates that the struggle over data in education was not so much about who should have the right to *produce* it as it was in the 1940s, but rather about how it should be *interpreted*. But with the kind of interpretation the left-wing educationalists made, they ended up with the conclusion that, considering the negative consequences of data in terms of reproduction of a society divided by class, it would be better if we did not measure outcome at all.

When the critics revealed that the promises of the government had not been fulfilled (by using the government's own data), the government had to realise that it had to use data in a more critical sense to understand the school system, and not just as a tool to regulate the system – because if not, others were willing to do so. In this way criticism was absorbed. The government started to promote local and national evaluations on a regular basis in order to get a better understanding of ongoing processes (Lundahl & Pettersson, 2010).

Student Resistance

Beginning in the late 1960s, there were also great protests against grades and testing from pupils. The pupil councils, who had formed a national organisation in the 1950s, expressed their criticism towards the norm-referenced grading system and national tests, and ultimately against all kind of grades, in national mass media (where they were frequently cited), in their own journals, in large demonstrations and strikes against the grading system and in boycotts against national tests. This protest movement of course mirrored wider tendencies in the late 1960s, where in particular young students at university expressed criticism against traditional social structures, but was also indicative of a change in the role of the pupil councils. Established in the 1930s and 1940s, the first pupil councils tended to be extremely loyal to the school and the teachers, and were mainly supposed to maintain discipline in schools. In the 1950s this gradually started to change, and the pupil councils acquired a role as organisations that were supposed to express the needs of the pupils. The pupil councils started to protest – against too much religion in school, against certain rules of conduct, against school books that were old-fashioned and so on. In the late 1960s the protests came to focus on the grading system, with demands for changing the norm-referenced grading system into a criterion-referenced grading system (e.g. Caspar & Jalander, 1969). In the 1970s this position was changed to demands for abolishing the grading system altogether. In 1977 a magazine called *Learn for Life – abolish grades*, printed in 600,000 copies, was distributed to all pupils in secondary school and upper secondary school, in a campaign that was described as 'the biggest political manifestation since the Vietnam demonstrations' (*Elevfront*, 1977, p. 1). In 1978 a demonstration against grades attracted 4000 participants, and in the newspaper article covering it, the head of the Pupils' Union said that public opinion was increasingly becoming sceptical towards grades: 'A growing number of people are joining the fight for a school without grades' (*Svenska Dagbladet*, 1978). However, the criticism by the pupils, so evident in the late 1960s and 1970s, became silent in the 1980s (Tholin, 2010). The pupil organisations were still critical of grades but they lost their voice in the mass media. Soon even this silent criticism would disappear, making pupil protests against grades a thing of the past. At the same time, it would be fair to claim that some of the principles in the norm-referenced grading system that the student organisations had criticised were slightly changed in the 1980s curriculum reform, partly due to the criticism (Lundahl, 2006).

The teacher and student movements of resistance resulted in some changes in the system of grading and national testing. They also led to reforms in *compensatory* instruction, special classes and so on. Overall, the government realised that the relationship between education and equality was more complex than at first stated (Hadenius, 1990). During the 1970s, the government and its educational agency started to produce a standardised *diagnostic test* to help teachers find students in need of extra support. The government also realised, from the 1980s, that it had to change curriculum standards, and move from a subject-oriented curriculum towards a more child-centred curriculum. Much of the standardised testing was fading away as a national discourse, but then in the late 1990s it suddenly returned.

Changing the School Paradigm:
the revival of standardised testing
and the death of resistance (1990-2012)

The last two decades have seen a paradigm shift when it comes to the role of data in Swedish schools. School inspection, international knowledge assessments and earlier grades in schools are among the new features of today's discourse on schooling. In order to illustrate how far public opinion has moved since the 1970s, we might start with a glance at one of the more radical voices of today. In the blog 'Revolutionary Communistic Youth' (*Revolutionär kommunistisk ungdom*), the question of grades was recently discussed. Since it is a radical left-wing publication, we might expect a radical perspective on grading. However, what is problematised is not grades in themselves, but the phenomenon of grade inflation. Grade inflation is described as a consequence of competition between municipal schools and free schools, and is said to lead to unfair grades. The fact that a revolutionary communistic organisation does not protest against the actual idea of grading pupils – but rather against how well the system functions – is not the only example of a fading resistance towards grades.

Since 2012 the grading system in Sweden has been changed in a way that stands out as both historically and internationally uncommon. In Sweden, grades used to be given from school year 8, but will from now on be given from school year 6. Given that the pupil organisations have a history of trying to abolish grades, we might expect that this radical change would be protested against. However, there have been no demonstrations, debate articles, books or other kinds of visible protests from pupil organisations. In fact, in 2010 the pupil organisations were asked for comments on the government bill circulated for consideration, but declined. The absence of protest against this reform testifies to the radical changes that have occurred since the 1970s. While the pupil organisations fought for schools without grades, the same organisations of today do not protest even when grades are given an increased role in schools. This absence of criticism was also exemplified when it comes to the introduction of standardised testing from grade 3. It passed without any critical reactions at all.

This does not mean that all kinds of resistance have disappeared. As Scott (1990) has argued, there is always a risk of exaggerating social hegemony if we do not take into account the fact of hidden resistance. While the collective, outspoken resistance of the 1970s is to a large extent gone, there are islands of resistance that have taken new forms. Individualised resistance that will help the pupil pass the test, help the teacher deal with the administrative workload or help the principal raise the status of the school are some examples of this (cf. Gilliom, 2010).

Synoptical Data: visualising failure and success

How can this radical shift from resistance to obedience be explained? One explanation is surely the position that data has come to occupy and the hopes and threats it raises. Data is today not something that simply works according to the panoptical principle, in which one watches the many. Increasingly, data is operating according to a synoptical principle, where a few watch many (cf. Mathiesen, 1997). On a global scale, numerous countries turn their heads towards Finland; on a national level the same things happen to the schools that receive prizes for high quality or increase their performance or in other ways prove successful. Everybody wants to look at the model, whether it is a foreign country, a municipality, a school, a teacher or a pupil.

This fascination with the success story coincides with repeated stories of educational failures. These stories have become easier to tell in the last few decades due to two innovations that have made failure easier to measure.

The first has to do with the disappearance of the norm-referenced grading system. The norm-referenced grading system normalised failure in the sense that the lowest grade were supposed to be given to 7% of school children. In 1994 a criterion-referenced grading system was introduced in Sweden. In the new grading system there were four grade levels: IG (fail), G (pass), VG (pass with distinction) and MVG (pass with special distinction). The new grading system contributed to making failure visible in a way that was not possible in a norm-referenced grading system. It made it easier to speak of the scandal of failing pupils, and also to set other, higher goals. This new way of thinking and speaking about schooling is well illustrated by a TV series about a school class that had its premiere in 2007, called *Class 9A*. It was a documentary which followed a school class, and ran for several episodes. The dramaturgy was simple: it was about turning a badly performing school class into an excellently performing school class. This dramatic transformation was achieved, or said to be achieved, with the help of 'star-teachers'. This concept can of course be seen as part of a wider trend where experts help amateurs achieve their goals, but must also be seen as an expression of new ways of speaking about schooling. The goal of the teaching in 9A was measured in a way that was impossible to measure before 1994: to ensure that most of the pupils did get the grade G (pass). Before 1994 the norm-referenced grading system made it impossible to create such goals. *Class 9A* was, in other words, a creation of a new way of thinking about schooling but it also contributed in disseminating that particular view of education, since it became a huge success, with many viewers, and since the 'star-teachers' became famous and often contributed in public debates about schooling. *Class 9A* consolidated the idea that schooling is about grades, and harmonised with current ways of describing what can be labelled as the scandal of schooling: that too many pupils do not reach the grade 'pass', which is a common complaint in journalism, political debates and general discussion about schooling today.

The second factor that has contributed to an increased focus on educational failure is international knowledge assessments. It has been argued that these show a decline in educational standards over recent years, and the fear that Sweden will lag behind has frequently been expressed. The fear of decline has repeatedly been used as an argument in discussions about schooling, discussions that are characterised by words such as 'crisis' and the need for more control, inspection and early assessment.

In Sweden, and other countries, we have seen a fervent effort to find the key to the success of the national school system that at the moment is the 'winning' one: the Finnish school. Based on statistics from the PISA studies, researchers, politicians, teachers and journalists all ask themselves the same questions about how the Finnish 'miracle' can be explained.

Since Finland is the major model country today – when it comes to education – it is fruitful to compare it with another model country from the past: the USA in the 1940s. When we compare the way that data has been collected from the respective countries and the conclusions that have been drawn from them, some really striking differences will be seen. Generalising a bit, the discourse on Finland can be said to exhibit the following features: 1. What is actually learnt in Finnish schools is seldom described. The success is supposed to be more or less apparent since Finland 'won' the PISA competition – the question is what can explain it. 2. The explanations of the success are to a large extent found on a political level. It is political steering – or the absence of steering, such as described by Sahlberg (2011) – that accounts for the success. 3. The idea of modernity is absent. Finland is not successful because it is modern. If anything, it is successful because it is traditional.

The new criterion-referenced grading system and the international assessments have made failure visible. They have created data that speaks the language of crisis. Paradoxically, they have also fed dreams of high performance. The 'world-class school' has become a vision that is often heard about (Figure 5). In this sense, the gap between visions and perceived reality has dramatically increased.

Figure 5. Delusions of grandeur in the era of crisis. This apple was produced by an advertising agency for the local educational department of Stockholm city. The text on the apple is written with laser and means 'a world-class school', which is the slogan that is used in educational policy for the schools of Stockholm.
Source: http://www.art4m.se/case/?caseid=4

Summary and Discussion

In this chapter we have explored the uses, meanings and consequences of data in Swedish educational reform, practice and discourse from roughly the 1940s up to the present. Our survey covers both national data and international data and includes quantitative as well as qualitative data. While this perhaps might seem a little too wide-ranging, it provides an opportunity to discuss the shifting ways in which the world of schooling has been represented, and raises important questions about why it is that certain data flourish during certain time periods.

To briefly summarise our argument: We started in the 1940s with two empirical examples that in a way showed an antithetical attitude towards data. The travel accounts from America were based on a qualitative approach, and expressed the attitude that the schools studied were important because they were different, modern and inspiring. At roughly the same time, standardised testing was introduced as a technique of connecting the different parts of the school system and rationalising the student admission processes. The consequences of this standardisation came under severe attack during the late 1960s and 1970s, resulting eventually in the introduction of a criterion-referenced grading system. Finally, we highlight the fact that the last few decades have seen the flourishing of such things as international assessment and school inspection, and there has been an increased emphasis on grades and testing. These examples illustrate that the meanings and techniques of data are objects of continuous negotiation. In order to grasp in what sense they represent different attitudes towards data, we will conclude with three observations on the nature of data and its shifting meanings.

Data Makes Comparisons Possible

The rise of standardised testing and grading was intimately tied to the democratisation of the school system and the creation of a common school for all. When all pupils were to be placed in the same institution, they had to be compared. After a couple of decades these standardised tests received much criticism, not least the norm-referenced grading system, that was considered to create excessive competition between the pupils. Although the grading system was changed into a criterion-reference grading system, the act of competition did not disappear. Today we can see that these processes have moved beyond the national border to the global arena. Even if large-scale international assessments aren't a new thing, their impact on national discourses has increased, as pointed out in 'No Country Left Behind' (Feuer, 2011). We have witnessed a massive globalisation of data, that in a sense could be described as a globalisation of the norm-referenced grading system. While PISA does not give grades to nations, it compares nations according to the same principles as pupils used to be compared, making education a zero–sum game. Further, the rise of international comparisons can be seen as the result of a global unification process that resembles the one that happened to the national school system in the 1940s. Just as the rise of standardised tests rested on the premise that the national school system was seen as a relatively homogenous entity, the PISA tests are based on the fact that no fundamental differences can be detected between nations; that different countries value student knowledge and achievements in similar ways. Numbers and statistics send a clear signal of comparability.

Data Changes the World

The aim of collecting data has normally been to change the world of schooling in some way or another. One way of putting this would be to say that data is a modernising force, but such a description arguably does not capture what is going on at the moment. Rather, we would argue that what is happening in Sweden could be described as the decline of data as a modernising force. This decline must be seen as a radical shift from what data used to mean. If we look at our first examples – on travel accounts and standardised testing – we see that these were imbued with a modernising spirit. They were about collecting inspiration from abroad from what was seen as the most modern school in the world, or about creating a national school system that previously did not exist. The same modernising spirit was part of the critique of the grading system of the 1970s. Today this idea of changing the world with data seems to be outdated. Data is rather a way of administrating the status quo at most (cf. Laïdi, 1998). Simplifying a little, we might distinguish between two strands in the pedagogical discourse: nostalgia about the 1970s and nostalgia about the 1950s. The most obvious example of this conservative modernisation is the fact that Finland, with its traditional school system, is today seen as an ideal model.

Data is Visible, and Therefore Possible to Criticise

While data is a visibility-making technique, it is also a fact that data in itself is visible. This means that, in contrast to the panoptical model of power, the uses of data do not imply the existence of an invisible surveillance that is impossible to criticise. Rather, the nature of data and its consequences are at least in principle possible to resist. The history of data in Swedish schools provides us with examples of trust and loyalty as well as mistrust and resistance towards different kinds of data. Although we ended with the observation that the resistance towards grades is today dead, there might in the future be other ways of showing resistance towards the way that data governs the world of education. An interesting example of how this resistance might look in the future can be found in Pasi Sahlberg's *Finnish Lessons*, a book that has been widely translated and read across the world. The argument that Sahlberg (2011) puts forward is based on the fact that some parts of the current data system are acknowledged, while others are not. The international comparisons of PISA are accepted as giving relevant information about schools in Finland, but the conclusion is that other kinds of data, such as New Public Management accountability data (from inspections and standardised testing), should be rejected. This is a rather ambivalent attitude towards data. Sahlberg uses data to fight data. Perhaps this (mis-)trust in numbers is a logical product of a society where everything is measured and where, consequently, even resistance towards measuring tends to be based on measurements.

Notes

[1] The title is inspired by Theodore Porter's book *Trust in Numbers* (1995), about how quantification gains legitimacy over expert judgements. By giving this phenomenon the prefix (Mis-), we will emphasise the conflicts embedded in the legitimation of numerical data.

[2] *Standardprov* (standardised tests) were introduced in order to individualise instruction and to calibrate teachers' grading of students. The principle behind norm-referenced grading is that every teacher compares his/her grading with the national normal distribution of 'test grades', and adjusts his/her grading according to this.

[3] In his thesis, Christian Lundahl (2006) describes the Swedish private teacher Gustaf Ruder (1708-71), who, between 1730 and 1750, wrote several books and pamphlets suggesting that external tests, based on the theory of the four temperaments, should be the guiding principle for selecting students to higher studies (*snillevalet*). The grammar schools were invited to write referrals on Ruder's suggestion. Their responses indicate that they did not see temperament theory as particularly problematic. The main problem from their perspective was rather that the decisions on students' performance and qualifications could not be based upon a single test or made by someone that had not followed the students' development for a long time.

[4] In Swedish *krut* is the word for gunpowder.

References

Alford, C.F. (2000) What Would it Matter if Everything Foucault Said about Prison Were Wrong? 'Discipline and Punish' after Twenty Years, *Theory and Society*, 29(1), 125-146.

Bauman, Z. (1989) *Modernity and the Holocaust*. Cambridge: Polity Press.

Boyne, R. (2000) Post-Panopticism, *Economy and Society*, 29(2), 285-307.

Callewaert, S. & Lundgren, U.P. (1976) Undervisningsforskning och social reproduktion, in S. Lundberg, S. Selander & U. Öhlund (Eds) *Jämlikhetsmyt och klassherravälde. En antologi om skola och utbildning i avancerade kapitalistiska samhällen.* Lund: Bo Cavefors Bokförlag.

Caspar, C. & Jalander, C. (1969) *Konkurrensskola* [Competition school]. Stockholm: Tiden.

Casserberg, T. (1948) *Social fostran i Amerikanska skolor* [Social education in American schools]. Stockholm: Svensk lärartidnings förlag.

Danziger, K. (1990) *Constructing the Subject: historical origins of psychological research.* Cambridge: Cambridge University Press.

Danziger, K. (1997) *Naming the Mind: how psychology found its language.* London: SAGE.

Doyle, E. (2011) Revisiting the Synopticon. Revisting Mathiesen's 'The Viewer Society' in the Age of Web 2.0, *Theoretical Criminology*, 15(3), 283-299.

Elevfront [Pupil front] (1977) Slaget om betygen har börjat [The battle against the grades has begun], 6/7, 1.

Feuer, M.J. (2011) No Country Left Behind: rhetoric and reality of international large-scale assessment. William H. Angoff Memorial Lecture. http://www.ets.org/Media/Research/pdf/PICANG13.pdf.

Gallagher, M. (2010) Are Schools Panoptic? *Surveillance & Society*, 7(3/4), 262-272.

Gilliom, J. (2010) Lying, Cheating and Teaching to the Test. The Politics of Surveillance under No Child Left Behind, in T. Monahan & R.D. Torres (Eds) *Schools Under Surveillance. Cultures of Control in Public Education.* New Brunswick: Rutgers University Press.

Gould, S.J. (1981) *The Mismeasure of Man.* New York: Norton.

Hadenius, K. (1990) *Jämlikhet och frihet: politiska mål för den svenska grundskolan.* Uppsala University. Stockholm: Almqvist & Wiksell.

Haggerty, K. (2006) Tear Down the Walls: on demolishing the Panopticon, in D. Lyon (Ed.) *Theorising Surveillance: the Panopticon and beyond.* London: Routledge.

Hägglund, S. (1990) *Skolmognad och skolstartsproblem i svensk grundskoleforskning* [School readiness in Swedish educational research]. META rapport no. 5. F 90:6/Vad säger forskningen? Stockholm: Skolöverstyrelsen.

Hermansson, E. (1940) *I amerikanska skolor* [In American schools]. Stockholm: Svensk lärartidnings förlag.

Husén, T., Björnsson, C.H., Edfeldt, Å.W. & Henrysson, S. (1956) *Betyg och standardprov. En orientering för föräldrar och lärare.*[Grading and standardised test. An introduction for parents and teachers]. Stockholm: Almqvist & Wiksell.

KRUT (1983) Fria folkhögskolestudier och centrala prov.[The folk high school and standardised test], no. 27/28. Image on page 67.

Laïdi, Z. (1998) *A World Without Meaning.* London: Routledge.

Lundahl, C. (2006) Viljan att veta vad andra vet. Kunskapsbedömning i tidigmodern, modern och senmodern skola [To know what others know. Assessment in education in pre-modern, modern, and late-modern times]. Dissertation, Uppsala University.

Lundahl, C. (2009) *Varför nationella prov? – framväxt, dilemman, utmaningar* [Why the national test – history, dilemmas, challenges]. Lund: Studentlitteratur.

Lundahl, C. & Pettersson, D. (2010) Den svenska skolans resultat. Från standardprov till PISA [The notion of results in Swedish education. From standardised test to PISA], in I E. Elstad & K. Sivesind (Eds) *PISA - sannheten om skolen?*, pp. 222-243.Olso: Universitetsförlaget.

Lundahl, C. & Waldow, F. (2009) Standardisation and 'Quick Languages': the shape-shifting of standardised measurement of pupil achievement in Sweden and Germany, *Journal of Comparative Education*, 45(3), 365-385.

Madaus, G.F. & O'Dwyer, L. (1999) A Short History of Performance Assessment – lessons learned, *Phi Delta Kappan*, 80(9), 688-696.

Mathiesen, T. (1997) The Viewer Society: Michel Foucault's 'Panopticon' revisited, *Theoretical Criminology*, 1(2), 215-234.

Myrdal, A. & Myrdal G. (1941) *Kontakt med Amerika* [Contact with America]. Stockholm: Albert Bonniers förlag.

Otter, C. (2008) *The Victorian Eye: a political history of light and vision in Britain, 1800-1910*. Chicago: The University of Chicago Press.

Porter, T.M. (1995) *Trust in Numbers: the pursuit of objectivity in science and in public life*. Princeton: Princeton University Press.

Sahlberg, P. (2011) *Finnish Lessons. What Can the World Learn from Educational Change in Finland?* New York: Teachers College Press.

SCB (1974) Elever i obligatoriska skolor 1847-1962 [Students in compulsory schools]. Promemoria Nr 1974:5.

Scott, J.C. (1990) *Domination and the Arts of Resistance. Hidden Transcripts*. New Haven: Yale University Press.

Skäringer-Larsson, E. (1941) *Demokratisk fostran I U.S.A.* [Democratic education in the USA]. Stockholm: Svensk lärartidnings förlag.

Sontag, S. (2001) *On Photography*. New York: Picador.

Svensk skoltidning [Swedish school magazine] (1963) Standardprov för årskurs 3 kommer i vår [Standardized tests for school year 3 will be introduced in spring], 13, 20-21.

Svenska Dagbladet [The Swedish daily] (1978) 4000 går mot betyg [4000 walk against grades], 14 May.

Tholin, J. (2010) Bilden av eleven i medias rapportering av betygsfrågor 1932-1990 och 2009 [The image of the pupil in media coverage of grade issues 1932-1990 and 2009], *Didaktisk tidskrift* [Journal of didactics], 19(1), 37-53.

Ydesén, C., Ludvigsen, K. & Lundahl, C. (2013) Creating an Educational Testing Profession in Norway, Sweden, and Denmark, 1910-1960, *European Educational Research Journal*, 12(1), 120-138.

Systems and Subjects: ordering, differentiating and institutionalising the modern urban child

IAN GROSVENOR & SIÂN ROBERTS

SUMMARY The chapter brings together two aspects of the modern experience: data gathering and the construction of the urban schooled child. It explores the ways in which knowledge about the urban child was created, collected, ordered and enlisted into the service of education (and welfare) policy making. The arguments presented here draw on data about the city of Birmingham, England.

The city in the nineteenth century became the quintessential site of modernity, the locus of the modern experience. It also moved to the centre of the concerns of the state about how the modern society was to be governed. This was especially the case in Britain, which, as Joyce (2003) observed, became simultaneously the world's first industrial state and its most heavily urbanised one. The dependence of the modern state, both locally and nationally, on the processes of surveillance, data collection and information ordering has engaged the research interests of historians, sociologists and cultural theorists (Tagg, 1998; Burke, 2000; Turmel, 2008). 'All states,' as Giddens observed, 'have been "information societies", since the generation of state power presumes reflexively monitored system reproduction, involving the regularised gathering, storage and control of information applied to administrative ends' (Giddens, 1985, p. 178). The nineteenth century also saw a shift in the west from education based on voluntary enterprise to a system where the state increasingly controlled the education of the urban child. Institutions, buildings and employees were designed and formed in a process by which cities created modern futures through the invention of the public sector. Education in the city was shaped and regularised through technology – a complex set of artefacts, actors and structures, and a set of socially constructed principles, procedures and processes, devised to function effectively and realise a purpose (Lawn, 1999). This purpose – a designed solution to mass schooling – was, according to Markus, social control:

> [control] is in the buildings which were adapted or purpose built, the space thus created, and the material contents of this space – furniture and equipment. Above all, it is in the order imposed on the human bodies in this space, down to their tiniest gestures, including the gaze of their eyes. (Quoted in Lawn & Grosvenor, 1999, p. 388)

The modern classroom was invented, together with a teacher, furniture, texts and aids, to produce a designed effect as a form of batch production (Hamilton, 1989). Pedagogic techniques and disciplinary practices developed in the classroom as 'technologies of government' (Donald, 1992). Children were viewed as the nation's future, although not all were assumed to be equal in delivering that future.

The aim of this study is to bring together these two strands of the modern experience: data gathering and the construction of the urban schooled child. The study will explore the ways in which knowledge about the urban child was created, collected, ordered and enlisted into the service of education (and welfare) policymaking. The arguments presented here will draw on data about Birmingham, England. Using Birmingham as a site of study in urban education is useful for two reasons. First, it has a history of urbanisation, industrialisation, de-industrialisation and technological change which can be viewed as representative of the metropolitan experience of Europe's capitalist commodity societies. Second, it has an extensive education archive, including individual school records from the nineteenth century onwards, architectural plans, education census data, photographs and local administrative records.

Focusing on the city of Birmingham but raising generic issues for urban centres in capitalist economies, the study is organised into four sections. In 'Knowing the City' the focus is on explaining the emergence of educational records in the contest of a civic revolution in which a new middle class sought to understand the world through the collection of data. The second section, 'Collecting Children', offers an analysis of the content of a range of educational records from the first half of the twentieth century. In the third section, using Latour's idea of 'centres of calculation' – social and epistemic spaces where local knowledge relating to children was assembled, recorded and catalogued – the circulation, exchange and utilisation of these records in a local system of surveillance is explored (Latour, 1999, pp. 24-79). In the final section, 'Archiving the City', the arguments around systems and subjects, and ordering, differentiating and institutionalising the modern urban child, are pulled together.

Knowing the City

In the 1860s Birmingham had become involved in a municipal renaissance which pushed it to the forefront of English cities. This civic revolution embraced education and Birmingham was one of the cities that took the lead in demanding 'the establishment of a system which shall secure the education of every child in the country' (Briggs, 1952, p. 101). This local revolution rested in part on a particular attitude to scientific knowledge that characterises the modern history of the city. This attitude can be best described as an acceptance of rationalist images of scientific knowledge and a commitment to its role in understanding particular social problems. It can be best explained by the vibrant presence of a scientific culture in Birmingham that, in turn, was an indication of the social position of marginal groups; dissenters and medics used science to develop and articulate an alternative value system that spoke to their marginality in wider society. Education and an emphasis on rational and practical knowledge was an integral element of that value system (Simon, 1974; Watts, 1998). The result was a city with a reputation in the nineteenth century for a certain scientific and religious radicalism. This radicalism was slowly legitimised by the incorporation of previously marginal groups in new elites. Birmingham's elite, as in other industrialising centres (Rueschemeyer & Skocpol, 1996), became increasingly concerned with the gathering of information about the lives, living conditions and moral education of the poor. Philanthropic and voluntary societies and literary and philosophical associations sought out data as a way of understanding perceived 'social problems' (Grosvenor & Myers, 2006). From the very beginning these societies and associations were much concerned with education. Since participation in particular forms of schooling was interpreted as a sign of moral probity and respectability, middle-class surveys routinely asked about educational attainment; about school attendance, literacy and ownership of reading materials. The Birmingham Statistical Society for the Promotion of Education, for example, founded in 1835, visited local schools in the early months of 1838 and gathered data on pupil numbers, age, number of school places and teachers, types of school, method of instruction, discipline and the curriculum. A report of their findings alongside comparative data for other cities was published in 1840 (Birmingham Statistical Society for the Improvement of Education, 1840). A comparative approach was also adopted by the Birmingham Natural and Philosophical Society in their 1895 report on Birmingham female pupil teachers. Influenced by eugenics and 'race-thinking', the Society used tests designed by Francis Galton to compare data with female pupil teachers in Boston, USA. The local middle class who had established and organised these societies and associations as a consequence of such data-gathering activities secured 'commanding knowledge' of their own town and strengthened their claim to local political leadership (Janes Yeo, 1996, p. 68). In other words, the new science of society was bound up with the rise of the new middle class who argued that objectivity in the investigation of social problems could only be secured by social distance (Collini, 1980). Knowledge about the social also involved the activities of middle-class women (Koven & Michel, 1993). Co-opted into knowledge production as social mothers, they were an important influence on policies that constructed and responded to the presumed needs of working-class mothers and children. By the turn of the twentieth century, knowledge creation became increasingly the preserve of education and child welfare professionals who, over the next 50 years or so, won a virtual monopoly over knowledge about the social; about the lives, living conditions and moral circumstances of urban children and their families.

Collecting Children

In this section five different Birmingham childcare records from the first half of the twentieth century are briefly described. They have been chosen because they all represent the process of 'child collecting', but are also very different in terms of the data collected, their intended audience and their form. They include a census book, a record card, an annual report, a research pamphlet and the report of a single professional.

The Education Census

The use of a census of children to generate data for local planning of school provision occurred intermittently in Birmingham from the late nineteenth century onwards. For example, a census was employed in 1874 to ascertain the amount of school accommodation needed in public elementary schools. The census as an investigative tool for particular inquiries was also utilised in the city. An Education Census, no longer extant, was undertaken in 1903 and involved the collection of data to identify 'all imbeciles, idiots, epileptics or feeble-minded' among 'children of school age' in Birmingham so that decisions could be made about provision and a second classificatory census of children attending schools for the 'mentally defective' was compiled in 1912. In 1907 the Local Education Authority (LEA) instituted a regular collection of census data and an Education Census was systematically undertaken in Birmingham from 1907 to 1970. The purpose of the census according to the LEA was 'for the enforcement of School Attendance Bye-Laws' and the regular revision of the census records 'ensure[d] that all children of school age were on roll at school' (Report of the Education Committee, 1941, p. 208). Birmingham was divided into districts and the data was collected by male School Attendance Officers (later termed Education Welfare and Attendance Officers), who annually systematically visited every house within the city boundaries. Today there are 4000 bound census volumes, each containing 201 numbered pages, in the City Archives. Entries are recorded on double pages (see Figure 1). The double pages are divided into printed columns. The average number of names recorded on a double page is 10, so a very basic calculation gives us a figure of 804,000 individual children entered into the record. For each child their age, address, school(s) attended, parents' names and occupation (usually only of the father) and a remark where the enumerator thought it appropriate are recorded in a column – so a minimum six pieces of information for each case, giving a total of 4,824,000 items of information.

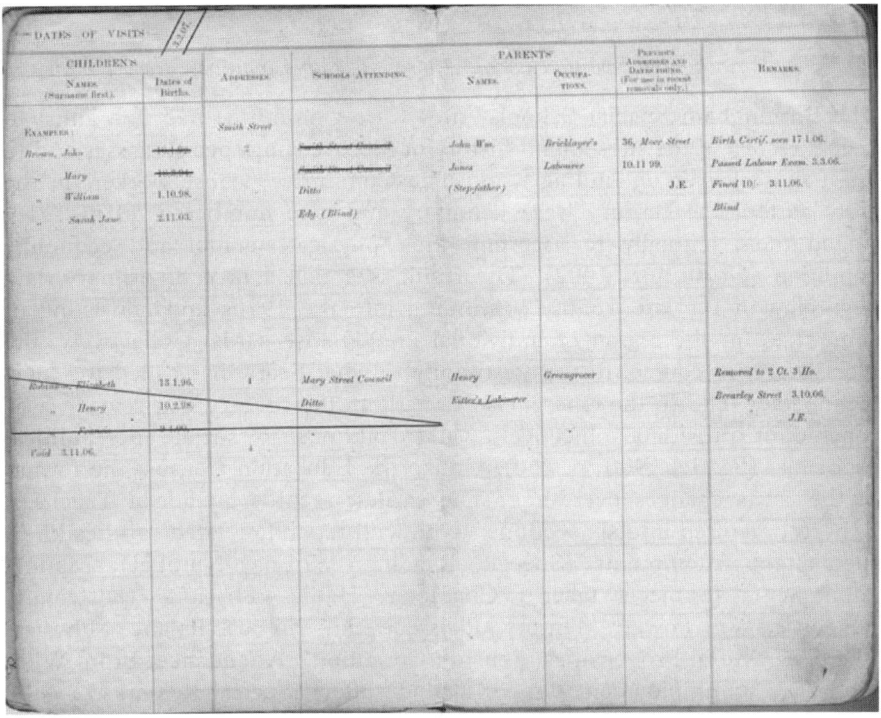

Figure 1. The Education Census.

While the format of the data collected remained constant throughout the period, local agendas about what additional details should be recorded did change over time. An earlier study of the content of comments made by the Officers revealed them to be actively engaged in a process of normalisation. The Officers visited each house on a regular basis and made judgements; they compared and differentiated in relation to assumed norms or standards of what was proper, reasonable, desirable and efficient. They visited, observed and, using reason, understood. They processed and categorised. The Officers appropriated into the record elements of a subject's history. Each individual was made into a documented case. Further, the record they produced provides profiles not only of individuals but also families, streets and communities. Cumulatively, the census provides a series of community dossiers. Moreover, these profiles are more detailed for working-class areas of the city as their homes received more frequent visits than those of Birmingham's middle-class citizens. In sum, the Welfare and School Attendance Officers recorded 'knowledge' of urban inhabitants which could be retrieved and referred to at any future point. Data was also aggregated on a weekly basis in a tabular form and circulated to relevant education officials in the city. The census books were superseded in 1969 by a card index system (Grosvenor, 2002).

The Birmingham Special Schools After Care Sub-Committee Record Cards

The Birmingham Special Schools After Care Committee had two aims: to keep a record of the subsequent history of those leaving special classes and to assist those leavers in finding work. The Committee, whose workers in the early part of the century were voluntary and who numbered 50 in 1913, visited them annually to ascertain their physical, mental and economic condition (Grosvenor, 2002). The result is a rich source of primary data beginning in the late 1890s, continuing into the 1970s and consisting of somewhere in the region of individual 28,000 case cards. Collectively, the records are, of course, further testimony to what Searle has called the 'new technocracy' and to the emerging idea early in the century that science 'was capable of providing objectively valid solutions to social and political problems' (Searle, 1990, p. 260). Unlike the Education Census, the format of the cards changes over time. The earliest records include a Teacher's Report, organised into six sections, some with separate related sub-headings: Elementary Attainments (Speech, Reading, Writing, Number); Manual Attainments (Subjects taken); Character, Habits, Physique (Discipline, Response, Will Power, Memory, Physique and Physical Balance, Physical Exercises, Moral Propensities, Sensory Condition); Attendance; From What hindrance to Employment does the child suffer?; Special Remarks. By the 1930s this element no longer has the heading Teacher's Report and the data columns have been simplified to: Appearance, Medical History, Physical Defects, Home Conditions, Conduct, Reading, Arithmetic, Mental, Writing, Manual and Diagnosis. Also by the 1930s the 'record' had expanded to several different cards: a basic data card including questions regarding attendance at Occupation Centres, membership of Social Clubs and 'trouble' with the Police; an education record card as described above along with a commentary on preparations for employment on leaving school; a Family History card for details of the individual's adult life, which required 'Remarks on Marriage'; and a card listing data gathered by 'after-care' visitors. Like the census books the cards carry the subjective opinions of the data collector(s) (Grosvenor & Myers, 2006).

School Medical Officer of Health Reports

The School Medical Service in Birmingham was established in 1908 to provide routine medical inspection of children in elementary schools (Body, 1928, p. 63). It is clear that, from early on, the collection of data was evidently central to effective Service performance. It had introduced an Epileptic Register 1911 and also a register of all children absent from school for prolonged periods. By 1928 the latter was changed to a card index system and recorded the names of every child who was away from school for three months, together with particulars as to the nature of the condition, and the treatment carried out so that the Service could exercise 'closer supervision' more 'immediately and systematically' and also work more effectively with the School Attendance Officers. The Epileptic Register continued in use, but the Chief School Medical Officer expressed disappointment in the same year that it was 'not possible to trace the after-histories of individual children' placed on the register (Birmingham City Council, 1928, pp. 9, 30; 1932, p. 9). The Second World War brought its own demands for additional data on children and the involvement of other agencies. So, for example, a questionnaire was sent by the School Medical Service in 1941 to 500 teachers in schools across the city to gather data on 'observable signs of nervousness or other disorders of conduct at school' and the Birmingham Society in Aid of Nervous Children was particularly concerned about the emotional state of boarded-out (fostered) children at this time (Birmingham City Council, 1949, p. 9).

There was a statutory requirement on local authorities to produce an annual report describing the work of the Service and the annual reports of the School Medical Officer were circulated to all in the School Medical Service, and to other related services within the Education Department. A copy of each report was also deposited with the City's Reference Library. In the 1935 report the Chief School Medical Officer, George Auden, noted that children were the object 'today' of 'all kinds of ad hoc examinations' including 'children for newspaper delivery, ... intending teachers, nutritional surveys, candidates for or recipients of free meals, ... children requiring remedial exercise treatment, or ultra-violet light, rheumatic clinics, ... candidates for all kinds of special schools ... [and] examination on leaving school' (Birmingham City Council, 1935, p. 8). Each of these examinations generated individual and aggregate child data.

The Present Problem of Juvenile Delinquency, 1938

Birmingham Education Committee in 1938 produced a small pamphlet about juvenile delinquency in the city (see Figure 2). The report had been prompted by concerns over the number of cases appearing before the Juvenile Courts in 1935 and 1936. Data was gathered about types of offences prosecuted, the type of schools attended by delinquents, their home conditions, family size and mental abilities. The findings were contextualised alongside data about London produced by Cyril Burt. The report concluded that although the number of offences had increased, much of the growth could be accounted for by the birth rate, alterations to age range, increased use of probation and the added interest in young offenders that had been prompted by the 1933 Children's Act. It went on however to note that 'some major disturbing element is to be found in most of the families producing delinquent children', the factors specifically mentioned being a deceased parent, unemployed father, working mother or a 'mentally defective' parent (Birmingham City Council Education Committee, 1938).

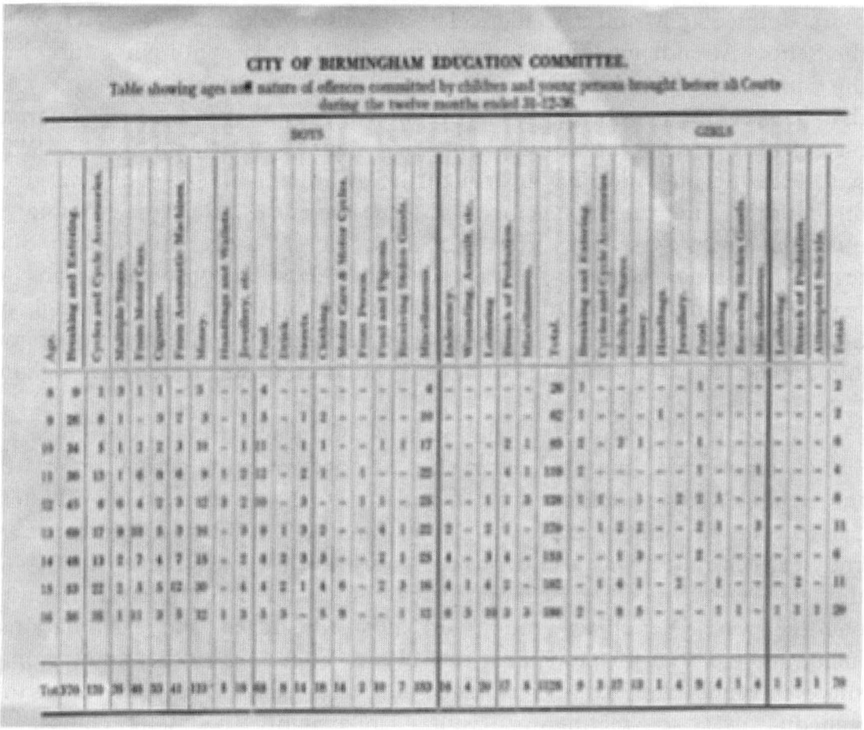
CITY OF BIRMINGHAM EDUCATION COMMITTEE.

Table showing ages and nature of offences committed by children and young persons brought before all Courts during the twelve months ended 31-12-36.

BOYS GIRLS

Figure 2. Table showing delinquent offences.
BCC Education Committee 'Problem of Juvenile Delinquency' 1938.

Report of Dr O'Brien on Her Visit to Europe, 1948

In 1948, as a consequence of national legislation, local authorities in England established children's departments which brought together professional knowledge which had previously sat in separate agencies. In the minute book of the Children's Committee, which oversaw the department's work, there is a record of an exploratory visit of Dr Margaret O'Brien of the City Public Health Department to Europe (see Figure 3).

```
                    HOLLAND
2nd April, 1948.    Arrived Amsterdam 11 a.m.
                    Visits to Dutch houses with Dr. van der Blink-
                                                         Roldor.

3rd    "      "     Visits to Residential Nursery and Home for
                    Unmarried Mother and Babies.

5th    "      "     Visit to Binnengasthuis (Children's Hospital)
                    Professor van Creveld.
                    Visit to Public Health Department - Dr. Dalmeyer,
                    Deputy Director of Public Health.

6th    "      "     Visit to Child Health Station and Open Air School
                    for delicate children - Dr. Dalmeyer.
                    Visits to (1) Orphanage (2) Day Nursery and
                    (3) Private Homes for (a) Protestant Children
                                          (b) Imbeciles.
                         Dr. van der Blink-Rolder.

7th    "      "     Day Nursery for delicate children - Dr. Blaauw
                                                         van Dok.
                    Mytyl School for Orthopaedic Children.
                    Child Guidance Clinic - Dr. Mulder.

8th    "      "     Arnhem - Day Nursery for delicate children, well
                    children and Toddlers Welfare Centre.
                    Johanna Stichting Orthopaedic After Care Home.
                    Oosterbeek. Convalescent Home for mentally
                    defective children.
                         Dr. Blaauw van Dok.

9th    "      "     R.C. Home for unmarried girls and their babies
                         Dr. van Gulden - Middelburg.
                    Infectious Diseases Hospital - Dr. Minkenhof.

10th   "      "     Children's Hospital.
                    Dr. Middelhoven; Professor de Lange,
                    Dr. Fiedeldy-Dop.

12th   "      "     Petten. Residential Nursery for foreschool
                    children, 3 - 6 years.
                    Bergen. Convalescent Home for School Children
                    6 - 13 years.
                         Sister Renecke.
                    Central Kitchen, Amsterdam.

13th   "      "     Public Health Department.
                    Dr. Neurdenberg - Statistician
                    Professor of Epidemiology.
                    Dr. Querido Director of Mental Hygiene
                    Children's Hospital - Professor van Creveld.
                    Laren - Home for war orphans, Professor van Creveld
                    Dr. Reitsema.

14th   "      "     Gerhard School - psychopathic children.
                    Yan Ligthart School - dull and retarded children.
                    Van Detschool - children with normal intellect
                    but partial defects.
                    Kingmaschool - for mongols and imbeciles
                         Dr. Meyers.

                    Noordweg. Willem van den Berg Colony for mental
                    defectives.
                         Dr. Querido

15th   "      "     Rotterdam. Children's Hospital.
                    Adriaan Stichting Orthopaedic Hospital and School.
                    The Hague. Children's Hospital.
                    Day Nursery for delicate children
```

Figure 3. O'Brien's Holland itinerary.

O'Brien visited Holland, Denmark, Switzerland, Sweden, Finland and Norway between April and June 1948. Her research agenda was to look at all aspects of childcare, but in particular provision for children who were illegitimate, neglected or deprived of parental care for any length of time. She undertook this knowledge-gathering project as a 'study leave' with support from the newly established Children's Committee. Within a month of her return to Birmingham she submitted to the Committee a 43-page report of her findings including details of relevant national childcare legislation and detailed itineraries for each country, institutions visited and the names of professionals she met. The length of her report reflected her need to share with the Committee the very different approach to childcare in these six countries, which she termed 'Social Paediatrics' (Birmingham City Council, 1949). O'Brien was not the first Birmingham professional to travel abroad to gather data. Auden, the School Medical Officer (1930-37), had paid extensive visits to schools and institutions in the USA in the 1930s to 'gain insight into the scope and methods of Medical Inspection and treatment' (Birmingham City Council, 1949). Deborah Thom (1992) has written about how the Commonwealth Fund in America paid for the Anglo-American exchange of Child Guidance staff in the 1930s. Such visits gave the observations and pronouncements of childcare professionals authority. Of course professional knowledge tourism was nothing new and had been a common feature of educational practice in the second half of the nineteenth century (Burke & Grosvenor, 2013).

Centres of Calculation, Dissemination and Exchange

The modern municipality's interest in her citizens extends from
the cradle to the grave; nay, even longer, from the ante-natal clinic
to the City cemetery, so carefully looked after when interest in the
erstwhile citizen is relinquished. (Body, 1928, p. 1)

The School Attendance Officers, the After Care Committee home visitors and the School Medical Officers all functioned within 'centres of calculation' where data relating to children was collected, stored and retrieved. These 'centres of calculation' collectively constituted in the urban landscape a complex medical-social-bureaucratic network of interconnected agencies, both statutory and voluntary. This network which brought individual professionals into contact (teachers, School Attendance Officers, Juvenile Welfare Workers, Probation Officers, Receiving and Remand Officers, Visitors of boarded-out children, tutors of Speech Classes, Health Visitors, Home Helps, Children's Court Magistrates, Educational Psychologists, Psychiatric Social Workers and representatives of a range of voluntary organisations such as the Children's Country Holiday Society, the Society for the Care of Invalid Children and the Society in Aid of Nervous Children) collected, stored and exchanged information about children and their families. As Shapin notes, 'knowledge of people was constitutively used to make and unmake knowledge of things' (Shapin, 1994, p. 287). Through their work and the records they produced, a child was subject to continuous regulation. Indeed, if a child attended a special school that regulation as indicated above could continue into adult and even married life (Myers & Brown, 2005; Grosvenor & Myers, 2006). As one School Medical Officer observed in 1936, 'future progress is likely to be in the direction of a closer co-operation on the part of all agencies working for the well-being of the child' (Birmingham City Council, 1936, p. 7).

The knowledge that was produced was exchanged within the network of agencies, but in the process of information exchange record types multiplied as data was inputted, extracted, reassembled and then circulated in a reconfigured form along a series of discrete information flows. Sometimes, the researcher can glimpse this process in operation, as records also functioned as a repository for other record types. Details of court orders relating to juveniles and transfers to the care of the Local Authority Children's Department in the 1950s can be found attached to pages in the Education Census books, and attendance cards for school clinic visits can be found stapled to the After Care Cards. One Education Census book consulted for the period 1954-67 contained over 10 attached memorandums and reports dated between 1954-68 on individual children covering home tuition, admittance to Special School, examinations at clinic, admission to hospital school and school exclusion (Grosvenor, 2002; Grosvenor & Myers 2006). Burke (2012) makes the important observation that, in the process of information circulation and exchange, there are 'intermediaries, gatekeepers and "epistemic brokers" who filter what they receive' and that, rather than one-way transmission, 'it is more useful to think of the circulation of knowledge in terms of "negotiation" of information and ideas or in terms of a dialogue' (Burke, 2012, pp. 86-87; see also Raj, 2006).

The ways in which data was presented also changed over time. The 'avalanche of printed numbers' (Hacking, 1990, p. 18) generated by data collection was increasingly transformed into tables, charts, graphs, maps and diagrams, which 'not only made the printed message clearer, but offered a substitute for it' (Burke, 2012, p. 102; see also Baigrie, 1996). Such 'visual inscription devices,' as Turmel has collectively described them, 'rendered the child visible' and offered the advantages to users of being more 'fathomable and intelligible ... mobile, immutable and reproducible' (Turmel, 2008, pp. 120-121). For example, the School Medical Officer Report for 1935 included a 'spot' map to indicate the distribution of children attending an open air school (see Figure 4). The map gave visual meaning to the city and the concentration of dots in the poorer inner city wards communicated quickly to the viewer the connection between child ill heath and environment. Similar connections were made in the 1938 *Problem of Juvenile Delinquency Report*, but here the connections are between inner city areas and the incidence of delinquency. The employment of visual inscription devices was driven both by the availability of new technologies of representation and by the need to present new kinds of material. The 1930s also witnessed an increased use of photographic evidence to sit alongside numbers, charts, graphs and text (Grosvenor & Hall, 2012).This interest in the use of the visual also extended to local authorities increasingly commissioning films to disseminate knowledge as a tool for urban and social reform (Lebas, 2011).

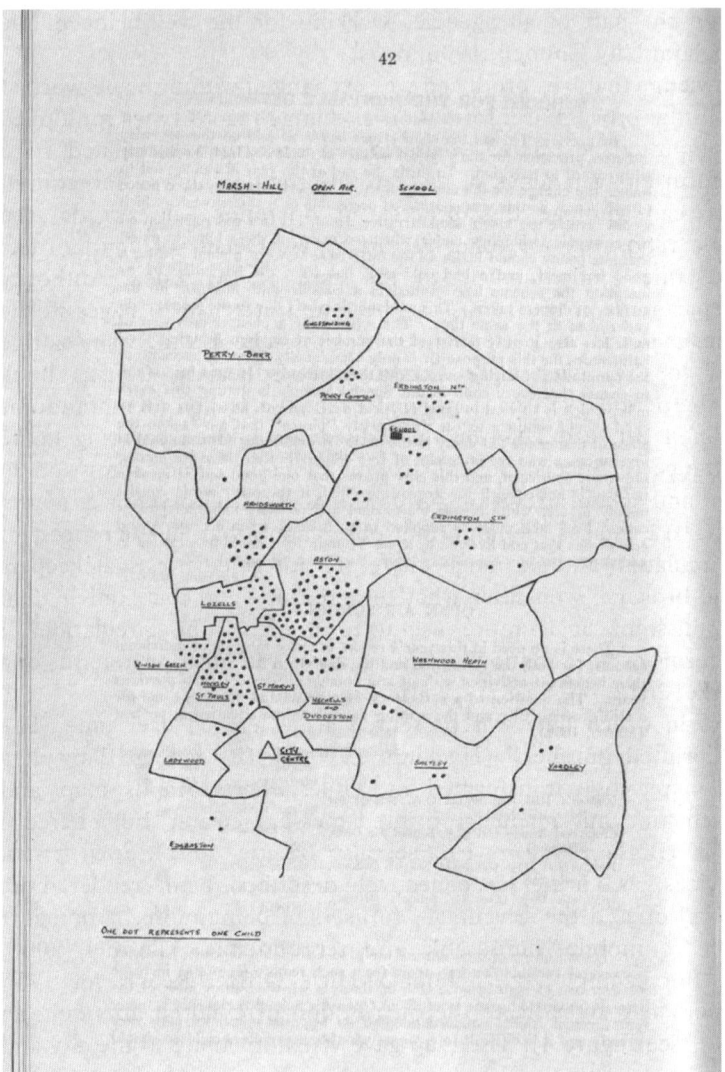

Figure 4. Distribution of children attending Marsh Hill Open Air School, 1935.

The medical-social-bureaucratic network of interconnected agencies, as it emerged and expanded over time, sat under and reported to an equally complex hierarchy of committees made up of elected local councillors, child professionals and administrators. To focus just on the education-related committees, in 1903 Birmingham City Council Education Committee was established with six standing sub-committees:

- Higher Education Sub-committee (secondary);
- Elementary Education Sub-committee (primary);
- Technical Education & Evening School Sub-committee;
- Special Schools Sub-committee;
- Sites & Buildings Sub-committee;
- Attendance Finance & General Purposes Sub-committee.

Over time these committees in turn spawned their own sub-sub committees:

- Higher Education Sub-committee (secondary) + one sub-sub-committee;
- Elementary Education Sub-committee (primary) + four sub-sub-committees;
- Technical Education & Evening School Sub-committee;
- Special Schools Sub-committee + five sub-sub-committees;
- Sites & Buildings Sub-committee + one sub-sub-committee;
- Attendance Finance & General Purposes Sub-committee + five sub-sub-committees.

By the 1940s the six standing sub-committees had increased in number to 10:

- 3 District School Managers Committees;
- Hygiene Sub-Committee + one sub-sub committee;
- The Continuation Schools Sub-Committee;
- The Juvenile, Employment and Welfare Sub-Committee + six sub-sub committees (Birmingham City Council, 2001).

Each of these committees commissioned and received knowledge generated by local officials and used it (or not) to inform and shape education and welfare policy (Foucault, 1980). This complex structure of education-related committees was, as stated earlier, reorganised as a consequence of the 1948 Children Act (Grosvenor, 2009, p. 233).

Sometimes the knowledge that was produced circulated to audiences beyond the city boundary. The 1938 School Medical Officer Report included a section on child nutrition in Birmingham, a local classification scheme and a discussion of the principle causes of malnutrition: 'pathological', 'financial' and 'social'. Five years later this data was reproduced in *Our Towns* (1943) as evidence of the condition of children in English towns and cities. This study, by the Women's Group on Public Welfare in association with the National Council of Social Service, reported on how evacuation of children during the war had brought to light the poor conditions of children in urban areas (Women's Group on Public Welfare, Appendix III). Not only had this data reached a wider audience, but in the process, to use de Certeau's concept of 're-emploi', it had been 're-employed' for a purpose not intended by the original collectors (de Certeau, 1980).

Archiving the City

> The archive is a dream of unity, of closure, of being able to grasp
> everything firmly and place it in a fixed position. Control of
> reality, of events, of possible meanings, attempted through control
> of information. (Wright, 1995, p. 45)

In *Birmingham and its Civic Managers* (1928), produced for the British Industries Fair, the Lord Mayor of Birmingham commended 'the plain and homely but inspiring record' of the work of the City Council and its committees to the citizens of Birmingham as 'a source of wonder and pride' and to a 'much wider circle of strangers within our gates' an 'interesting resume of our methods of municipal management' (Body, 1928, 'Foreword'). Central to the success of Birmingham's civic administration in the first half of the twentieth century was the collection, analysis, dissemination and employment of knowledge about the city's inhabitants.

This study, using the records of Birmingham, has shown how the modern local state became involved in the systematisation of knowledge, in the compiling, checking, synthesising and methodising of new information so that knowledge was produced. The city was confident and systematic about what it needed to know about itself. In the field of education, counting children and assessing their educational needs was designed to promote the provision of efficient and appropriate schooling for all. It aimed to make the population more visible and its documentation of social, economic and environmental problems was understood as a necessary stage in their resolution. City children were governed through a range of people, places and hubs of information. They were seen in new ways, made visible through new means and managed through new systems and networks. Their lives, families and communities, in other words their place in the city, are revealed through the records and reports. Data was recorded and judgements were made about individual children and their families. The knowledge of individuals so produced was fed 'into knowledge of aggregates' whereby 'governance through collective and "social" subjects deepened' (Joyce, 2003, p. 21); however, the individual judgements were secretive, remained exclusively in policymaking and professional circles and so were never seen or controlled or disputed by the objects of attention. These records therefore constituted part of an extensive system of population surveillance that was both secretive and exclusive and had significant implications for both citizens and city. The study has also tried to flesh out some of the data flows between departments, occupations and individuals and how, in the process, information was amended, supplemented and reconfigured. The various charts, graphs and maps operated as 'mediators/translators' (Turmel, 2008,

p. 119) within a complex institutional framework of disciplinary authorities, making the child visible in the city and enabling decisions to be made and enacted.

Finally, what then of the records created, collected and stored in the process of 'archiving the city' in the first half of the twentieth century? There is a sense, particularly when reading the Education Census volumes, that, because they were part of a large-scale data set, they developed an organic life of their own with details which would never inform policy or practice being slavishly gathered and kept. In time, they became for the organisation that produced them a burden from the past, the 'scientific' knowledge contained within them no longer deemed relevant and elements of their purpose and meaning obscured. Indeed, 'caring for the past' as the city planned for the future was seen as a problem for the city in the 1970s, as the Finance and General Purposes Committee reported:

> [the Education Committee] has neither adequate facilities nor qualified staff for the care of these records ... They are at present scattered between the basement of 102 Edmund Street, a Committee Room, offices, stock rooms and strong rooms in the Education Office, and a stock room in the Art and Design Centre of the Polytechnic. The lack of systematic cataloguery and storage in the past has been shown by the chance discovery of missing volumes of sets of minutes kept by one Branch in odd cupboards or with records kept by a different branch of the Department; in spite of further searches some sets of records are still incomplete. (Birmingham City Council, 1973)

Nevertheless, what has survived enables historians to explore and understand how the city attempted 'to grasp everything firmly' about its inhabitants and to place them 'in a fixed position' and, in the process, observe how archiving the city contributed to the legitimisation of a 'science of childhood' (Turmel, 2008, p. 121).

References

Baigrie, B.S. (Ed.) (1996) *Picturing Knowledge*. Toronto: Toronto University Press.

Birmingham City Council (1928) *Annual Report of the School Medical Officer*. Birmingham: Birmingham City Council.

Birmingham City Council (1932) *Annual Report of the School Medical Officer*. Birmingham: Birmingham City Council.

Birmingham City Council (1935) *Annual Report of the School Medical Officer*. Birmingham: Birmingham City Council.

Birmingham City Council (1936) *Annual Report of School Medical Officer*. Birmingham: Birmingham City Council.

Birmingham City Council (1949) Children's Committee minutes, Report of Dr. O'Brien of City Public Health Dept. visits to Holland, Norway, Denmark, Sweden, Switzerland, Finland, 1948. Birmingham: Birmingham City Council.

Birmingham City Council (1973) Finance and General Purposes Sub-Committee, Report of Chief Education Officer on Records and Publications in the Care of the Education Committee, 16 November.

Birmingham City Council (2001) *The City a Light and a Beacon: a guide to Birmingham education archives.* Birmingham: Birmingham City Council and History of Education Society (UK).

Birmingham City Council Children's Committee Minutes, No 1, 7 July 1948-3 May, 1949, Birmingham Libraries & Archives BCC 1/CT/1/1/1.

Birmingham City Council Education Census records, Birmingham Libraries & Archives BCC 1/BH/D/1/1/3/2.

Birmingham City Council Education Committee (1938) *Problem of Juvenile Delinquency.* Birmingham: Birmingham City Council.

Birmingham City Council Special Schools After Care Sub-Committee Record Cards, Birmingham Libraries & Archives BCC 1/BH/D.

Birmingham Statistical Society for the Improvement of Education (1840) *Journal of Statistics,* 3, pp. 25-29, Birmingham Libraries & Archives MS 1683/2.

Briggs, A. (1952) *History of Birmingham. Volume II Borough and City 1865-1938.* Oxford: Oxford University Press.

Body, W.S. (Ed.) (1928) *Birmingham and its Civic Managers. The Departmental Doings of Birmingham City Council.* Birmingham: Stanford and Mann.

Burke, C. & Grosvenor, I. (2013) An Exploration of the Writing and Reading of a Life: the 'body parts' of the Victorian school architect E.R. Robson, in T.S. Popkewitz (Ed.) *Rethinking History of Education. Transnational Perspectives on Its Questions, Methods, and Knowledge,* pp. 201-220. New York: Palgrave Macmillan.

Burke, P. (2000) *A Social History of Knowledge from Gutenberg to Diderot.* Cambridge: Polity.

Burke, P. (2012) *A Social History of Knowledge II from the Encyclopédie to Wikipedia.* Cambridge: Polity.

Certeau, M. de (1980) *L'Invention du quotidien.* Paris: Gallimard.

Collini, S. (1980) Political Theory and the 'Science of Society' in Victorian Britain, *The Historical Journal,* 23(1), 203-231.

Donald, J. (1992) *Sentimental Education.* London: Verso.

Foucault, M. (1980) *Power/Knowledge: selected interviews and other writings 1972-1977.* Brighton: Harvester Press.

Giddens, A. (1985) *A Contemporary Critique of Historical Materialism. Vol. 2. The Nation-State and Violence.* London: Polity.

Grosvenor, I. (2002) 'All the Names': LEAs and the making of pupil and community identities, *Oxford Review of Education,* 28(2&3), 299-310.

Grosvenor, I. (2009) Geographies of Risk: an exploration of city childhoods in early twentieth century Britain, *Paedagogica Historica,* 45(1&2), 215-233.

Grosvenor I. & Hall, A. (2012) Back to School from a Holiday in the Slums! Images, Words and Inequalities, *Critical Social Policy*, 32(1), 11-30.

Grosvenor, I. & Myers, K. (2006) Progressivism, Control and Correction: Local Education Authorities and educational policy in 20th century England, *Paedagogica Historica*, 43(1&2), 225-248.

Hacking, I. (1990) *The Taming of Chance*. Cambridge: Cambridge University Press.

Hamilton, D. (1989) *A Theory of Schooling*. Lewes: Falmer Press.

Janes Yeo, E. (1996) *The Contest for Social Science: relations and representations of gender and class*. London: Rivers Oram Press.

Joyce, P. (2003) *The Rule of Freedom*. London: Verso.

Koven, S. & Michel, S. (Eds) (1993) *Mothers of a New World: maternalist politics and the origins of welfare states*. London: Routledge.

Latour, B. (1999) *Circulating Reference: sampling the soil in the Amazon forest in Pandora's Hope: essays on the reality of science studies*. Cambridge, MA: Harvard University Press, 24-79.

Lawn, M. (1999) Designing Teaching: the classroom as a technology, in I. Grosvenor, M. Lawn & K. Rousmaniere (Eds) *Silences and Images. The Social History of the Classroom*, pp. 63-82. New York: Peter Lang.

Lawn, M. & Grosvenor, I. (1999) Imagining a Project: networks, discourses and spaces – towards a new archaeology of urban education, *Paedagogica Historica*, 35(2), 381-394.

Lebas, E. (2011) *Forgotten Futures. British Municipal Cinema 1920-1980*. London: Black Dog Publishing.

Markus, T. (1996) Early Nineteenth Century School Space and Ideology, *Paedagogica Historica*, 31(1), 9-50.

Myers, K. & Brown, A. (2005) Mental Deficiency: the diagnosis and after-care of special school leavers in early twentieth century Birmingham, *Journal of Sociology*, XVIII, 72-98.

Raj, K. (2006) *Relocating Modern Science: circulation and the construction of knowledge in South Asia and Europe, 1650-1900*. London: Palgrave Macmillan.

Report of the Work of the City of Birmingham Education Committee 1941. Birmingham: Birmingham City Council.

Rueschemeyer, D. & Skocpol, T. (Eds) (1996) *States, Social Knowledge and the Origins of Modern Social Policy*. Princeton, NJ: Princeton University Press.

Searle, G.R. (1990) *The Quest for National Efficiency: a study in British politics and political thought, 1899-1914*. London: Prometheus Books.

Simon, B. (1974) *The Two Nations and the Educational Structure 1780-1870*. London: Lawrence & Wishart.

Shapin, S. (1994) *A Social History of Truth: civility and science in seventeenth-century England*. Chicago: Chicago University Press.

Tagg, J. (1988) *The Burden of Representation. Essays on Photographies and Histories*. Basingstoke: Macmillan.

Thom, D. (1992) Wishes, Anxieties, Play and Gestures. Child Guidance in Inter-War England, in R. Cooter (Ed.) *In the Name of the Child. Health and Welfare, 1880-1940,* pp. 200-219. London: Routledge.

Turmel, A. (2008) *A Historical Sociology of Childhood.* Cambridge: Cambridge University Press.

Watts, R.E. (1998) *Gender, Power and the Unitarians in England 1760-1860.* London: Routledge.

Windle, B.C.A. & Manners-Smith, T. (1895) On the Physical Characteristics of a Group of Birmingham Pupil Teachers (Female). *Proceedings of the Birmingham Natural and Philosophical Society,* 9, part 2, n.p.

Women's Group on Public Welfare (1943) *Our Towns. A Close Up.* London: Oxford University Press.

Wright, C. (1995) *Dialogues between Anthropology and Photography.* London: Photographers' Gallery.

Counting, Describing, Interpreting: a study on early school census in Argentina, 1880-1900

INÉS DUSSEL

SUMMARY The chapter analyzes the emergence of educational data in Argentina at the end of the nineteenth century. It focuses on the first educational census from 1883 to 1884 and the institutional history of educational statistics in that country, as well as on the peculiar trajectory of one of its leading figures, Francisco Latzina. Grounding on science studies and histories of statistics, it looks at the categories and narratives that were used in the census and adjacent reports. It presents the history of educational data as an institutional and epistemological production that, while nationally set, was part of an international network that brought forth a new language for understanding and governing education.

In our times, it is superfluous to value statistics as an instrument of scientific research, because all human physical acts are reduced in their origin to measure, weight and count ... Statistics is an organ through which society instructs itself about the conditions of its existence. Neither the sociologist nor the economist or the politician can do without its teachings, under the penalty of wandering in vacuum. (Latzina, 1914, p. 527)

Even if expensive and even unpleasant to fill pages with numbers, publishing facts pays a better service to science than publishing the interpretations and doctrines that are made out of them. (Mercante, 1918, p. 121)

Since at least the end of the nineteenth century, numbers have been considered a theory-free and value-free category. Calls for counting and measuring are heard everywhere in educational systems, be it for valuing the learning of students, the work of teachers, or the level of adoption of ICTs.

Numbers seem to provide the magical key to understanding life, reality, 'the facts'.

But, as Lorraine Daston said, the factual too has a history, and it needs to be problematized (Daston, 1991). How could numbers get to be thought as separable and distinct from interpretations and doctrines? How were they produced as untheoretical, impartial and transparent conveyors of the conditions of existence? Both Latzina, whose work will be discussed at length in this chapter as one of the main statisticians in Argentina in the second half of the nineteenth century, and Mercante, a renowned psychologist who initiated experimental psychology and pedology in the same country, believed that numbers gave direct entry to the world in ways that theories or interpretations did not. They are the precursors of today's faith in numbers.[1]

But things could have been otherwise, and this chapter would like to discuss those possibilities. Despite their claims, neither Latzina nor Mercante could do without interpretations, and statistics was also a 'constructed (and possibly unstable) amalgam of practices' (Poovey, 1998, p. xiv). This text deals with the emergence of educational data in Argentina during the last decades of the nineteenth century. Through analysis of the first national educational census from 1883-84, I would like to describe the categories and languages used to account for educational processes, and which would later become what is now known as educational data. This moment signals a transition from a language of description through *types* or picturesque rhetoric (common among education reports, topographers and travel writing in the nineteenth century, cf. David, 2003), to a language of description based on observable facts, generally expressed through numerical and standardized categories. But there persisted an ambivalence in the statistical reports about abstractions and masses that eventually resorted to the narratives and rhetorics that it intended to surpass.

Numbers are particular kinds of inscriptions, and produce traceable phenomena that can travel across time and space. The introduction of statistical language through the census and record keeping by schools intended to make education visible and manageable, and also comparable on a national and international level. This was linked to the expansion of governmentality: the machinery of the state was 'indissolubly tied to the collection of numerical information' (Poovey, 1998, p. 317; see also De La Peña & Wilkie, 1994; Larsen, 2004). The grid of visibility allowed the centralization of power and the control of the population, even the creation of kinds of people that came to be seen and spoken of in specific terms (Hacking, 1995).

It was a time when 'an almost magical power was given to the language of numbers' (DePaepe, 1992, p. 75). But what I would like to discuss in this chapter is that what was considered as 'numbers' had to be stabilized, and there were shifts and displacements in terms both of the 'technicality' of numbers (the domain of statisticians) and of the social categories with which to account for the social (the domain of sociologists, politicians and also educators). The collection of 'raw data' done by statisticians relied on the categories and interpretations of childhood, literacy, schooling, race, and class constructed by the theorists.

It was also a time when the separation between the language of description – numbers – and the language of interpretation – narratives – seemed more acute, although it had been initiated a long time ago.[2] However, during the second half of the nineteenth century, numbers did not circulate isolated but were part and parcel of narratives about schooling. When looking at reports, there is an appeal both to numbers and to narratives. Numbers seemed to be 'both essential and insufficient' in themselves (Poovey, 1998, p. xi). There was no complete and total rupture between the two modes of representation. Numbers, and the narratives that supported them, organized what was to be seen, how it was to be seen, by whom, and who could present it as table or a chart that conveyed the facts. Numbers provided a centralized visuality from above, a complete map, as in the panorama described by Latour (2005), but these inscriptions had to be produced through particular languages that combined numbers and stories in different ways. How were these languages stated, and by whom? This chapter intends to discuss some of these issues through a historical analysis of early educational statistical reports from Argentina.

My analysis is grounded on the works of Mary Poovey (1998), Lorraine Daston (1991) and her production with Peter Galison (2007), and Latour (2005), which can be grouped in what is called science studies. These authors have produced remarkable histories of scientific observation, of the notions of objectivity, or of the factual – a historical epistemology (Poovey, 1998, p. 7). In particular, Poovey's book on the history of the modern fact has inspired some of my questions. For Poovey, the modern fact is an epistemological unit that consists of numerical descriptions, apparently noninterpretive, yet at the same time acts as the bedrock of systematic knowledge that relies on theoretical assumptions that it seems (and promises) to leave behind (Poovey, 1998, pp. xi-xiii). She remarks that there was no necessary connection between 'the modern fact and numbers as a specific form of representation': there were numbers that acted separately from any idea of a systematic knowledge, such as the numbering of paragraphs in the Bible or books, and there were facts that were not numerical, such as the cataloguing of herbs that was produced in the sixteenth century (Poovey, 1998, p. 5). The modern fact produced a way of doing research but also looking at the world that allowed to consider particulars that could be observed and quantified (thus numbers), and that at the same time were subordinated to abstractions that could not be seen (as population or market).

Also, histories of statistics (De La Peña & Wilkie, 1994; Dodier, 1996; Otero, 1998, 2006; Desrosières, 1999; Díaz, 2003) are important referents for understanding the development of a disciplinary and social field. These texts show the extent to which educational data has to be understood at the crossroads of bureaucracy and state making, the emergence of social sciences and expert knowledge on social issues, and political rationalities that mobilized arguments in one direction or the other.

The chapter is organized in four sections. The first one provides a brief account of the emergence of official statistics, and sets the stage for understanding some of the institutional context of Argentinean statisticians. The second discusses early educational statistical reports, and the third focuses on the school census from 1883-84. The fourth section discusses the reports written to interpret the results. The final section provides some concluding remarks that probably leave more questions opened than answered.

The Emergence of Official Statistics

The process of turning educational statistics into the most accurate representation of reality, and into a powerful means of intervention and mobilization in educational policies, was long and not devoid of controversies. During the nineteenth century,

> [n]ew authorities were established to classify, enumerate and
> tabulate subjects for the purposes of taxation, military recruitment
> and in some cases, political representation. The most significant of
> these new technologies were the statistical bureaus created by a
> range of wide range of western nation states, each unique in its
> own way, although paralleling each other across North America,
> Europe and Great Britain. (Larsen, 2004, p. 3)

As Alain Desrosières shows, this was a process that was both national and international. To have a statistical bureau was, for many of the European states, and even more so for Latin American countries, a sign of modern, rational administration. But it was also a way of creating a nation, of rendering local observations homogeneous, of creating common patterns and categories to measure reality and to produce a narrative around them. 'Statistics do not merely "reflect" national reality but also "establish" it, in the same way as the Constitution, national holidays, anthems, flags, school textbooks, and historical monuments' (Desrosières, 1999, p. 4). Nations projected themselves in the numbers that gave them a sense of progress and growth that nurtured national imaginaries.

At the same time, this was an international movement, propelled among others by a new breed of scientists who believed in the universal quality of knowledge, and whose action was important in Argentina. In statistics, the Belgian Quetelet (1796-1874) promoted international congresses that, at least for a while, brought together politicians, statisticians, mathematicians and educators. While these congresses could not survive the increasing hostility among European nations by the end of the nineteenth century, they nonetheless contributed to the creation of the International Statistical Institute, the first international agency in the field.

In Argentina, the first Office for National Statistics was created in 1864 but was closed in 1874 due to lack of funds, and its functions transferred to the Ministry of Finance and the National Direction for Immigration (Otero, 2006, p. 182). At the time of its creation, there was significant debate about whether this Office was needed given that there were officials at the provincial (local) level whose task was to collect data and send it to the national authorities. However, in 1869, 1876 and 1880, the federal government claimed that the data collected was poor and incomplete, and that further centralization and professionalization was needed. Despite the weak institutionalization, in the 1890s a Law for National Statistics was passed and the discipline achieved greater consolidation.

During those interim years, there were also Statistical Bureaus at the provincial levels and, through these institutions, a network of 'state scientists' emerged that became specialized in statistics. Statisticians were to be a professional body that assumed the task of producing or collecting 'raw data', and in many cases left to others (sociologists, politicians) the interpretation of results (Poovey, 1998). This division of labor did not quite happen in Argentina, at least not in the time considered in this text: the statisticians produced the evidence but also the interpretation, and went back and forth from policy making to technical decisions.

The Office for National Statistics organized the first Census in 1869, quite early in the international context. According to Hernán Otero, a historian of Argentinean statistics, the Census established some criteria that were to last until 1947, when the fourth Census was taken. Among them, the consideration of individuals and not families (as the colonial administration had done), and the adoption of the concept of 'de facto population', which counts only the individuals present at the moment of the survey (Otero, 2006, p. 186). These technical criteria were up to date with international debates and persist to this day. The design of the data collection was inspired on the American structure, although it differed on not choosing self-administration of the survey. There were to be a National Commission and Provincial Boards, which would hire public employees, teachers, or 'enlightened, moral and active citizens', preferably nationals but, if these were not available, foreigners would do too (Otero, 2006, p. 189). The Census was not entirely successful, as there was a high level of non-respondents for political reasons (the country was still in the midst of a civil war and the fear of a military levy was much present; also, the frontier with the aboriginal tribes was not stabilized and what constituted the national territory was hotly debated). However, Argentineans took great pride in being pioneers in the field and actively participated in international networks, as it will be seen in the next section.

101

Counting and Measuring in Education

Educational statistics, as the counting of individuals and population movements around schools, began in at least 1822, when a decree was passed that obliged every teacher to report the number of students s/he received (Díaz, 2003, p. 50). This requirement was related to the establishment of a centralized educational system that copied the Napoleonic University and put the Department of First Letters under the rule of the university.

But the political instability of the country made it difficult to consolidate these practices. It would be in the second half of the nineteenth century that modern systems of statistics would appear, and – as seen before – they were not set for a steady march.

I would like to focus my analysis on the work of one of the 'state scientists' described by Otero: Francisco Latzina, who would be later the director of the National Bureau for Statistics from 1880 to 1916. His life history is representative of this breed of nineteenth-century international scientists who did not separate science from intellectual and political affairs.

Latzina (1843-1922) was born in Moravia and had served in the Austro-Hungarian Navy, where he learned mathematics. He was also versed in astronomy, as was the Belgian Quetelet. He immigrated to Argentina on an unknown date, but the earliest records of his actions in this country are from 1872, when he was hired to teach mathematics at the National College (*baccaulauréat*) in a northern province, Catamarca, where he also taught at the School of Mines. He later moved to a central province, Córdoba, where he joined the recently created Astronomical Observatory, and the new School for Physical-Mathematical Sciences in the National University of Córdoba (1876). He was also very active as a geographer, and published a geographical atlas of the Argentine Republic with detailed maps of the territory.

Latzina was part of a group of foreigners who participated in the creation of scientific institutions that had strong ties with international networks.[3] He was a member of the International Society of Statistics from Paris, the Royal Statistical Society, and the International Institute of Statistics (Otero, 2006, p. 195). He traveled to international meetings and kept current with technical and political debates. Science was an international field, a cosmopolitan discipline that should follow the same lines. But it was also a national affair: he promoted the passing of the Law that created a new, more modern National Direction of Statistics in 1894.

Latzina thought that there were four pillars in the progress of the nation: foreign trade, state assets, agriculture and farming, and schooling. He contributed to the creation of quantitative measures to follow these dimensions, and he became particularly involved in education.

In 1877, Latzina produced a report on the state of education in four provinces from the center and eastern part of the country (Córdoba, Santa Fe, Entre Ríos and Corrientes), for which he visited 598 schools, of which 136 private. His report organized several of the categories that were later used in the first National Census in 1883-84. The data he collected was gathered at the schools themselves, and included not only the children who regularly attended the schools but also many dimensions of schooling: buildings, instructional materials, and subjects taught.

Based on these categories, he found that the state of education in these provinces was very poor (again, numbers did not circulate alone but were tied to narratives, in this case of failure or poor progress). For example, of the 598 schools, only 52 owned their buildings; the rest rented theirs. He counted 26,543 students, and only 5827 benches and desks. Latzina interpreted this disparity as a result of the negligence of authorities to provide for equipment, but it could be hypothesized that not all children attended schools regularly. In many parts of his report, and despite the constant use of statistical numbers, the reader is provided with an interpretation that asks for the kind of 'leaps of faith' Mary Poovey refers to.

He surveyed the kind of instructional materials that the schools used: 55% of the schools had blackboards, 40% had wall charts or pictures, 10% had wall maps, 17% had globes, and 10% had geometrical sets. He asked about the subjects taught in schools, as in full awareness of the distance between the prescribed curriculum and school teaching. The results are interesting for a history of curriculum: 94% of schools taught reading and writing, but only 73% taught grammar; 83% taught arithmetic; 51% taught national geography and 39% national history; only 10% taught geometry and drawing.

Latzina had the expert's eye for data. On the one hand, he surveyed whether the schools were keeping records of students' attendance and performance, and he found that, out of 598 schools, only 45 did it. 'All depends on the memory of the teacher, and as they change constantly in search of a better job, there is no reliable record' (Latzina, 1885, p. 121). This evidenced the fragility of the system: there was no way of keeping track of students' movement across schools or of collecting uniform data about schools. It was the panoramic view that made him see what was missing in this state of affairs. In his report, Latzina advocated for a professionalization of data collecting and for forcing the schools into record keeping.

The teachers' situation was another dimension that Latzina looked at closely. He talked about this in a political way: 'Good teachers are the basic need of teaching; the better the teacher, the better the school, and good teachers are not available if poorly paid' (Latzina, 1885, p. 121). The reference to payment and working conditions stands out in a report commissioned by the authorities, but Latzina played the scientific, 'neutral' card to mingle with educational policy.

> One of the consequences of a poor and irregular payment is that no system of opposition (aggrégation) can be established ... The recruitment of teachers is thus made among unemployed persons without the knowledge or the vocation to become a teacher, and who use teaching as a step toward a more rewarding job. From

there it follows that school personnel, methods and habits are perpetually changing, discipline and moral loosen, and the last fruit of this genre of instabilities is the null benefit for the students. (Latzina, 1885, p. 121)

The fact that there were 854 teachers for 26,543 students did not shock him as much as the fact that almost 40% of them were foreigners. Nationality was a great issue at that time in Argentina, as will be shown later, and this seems to have passed through even to foreigners such as Latzina.

The First School Census: children as a population category

Some years later, Latzina organized the First School Census (Censo Escolar, 1885). Mandated by the Parliament by the end of 1883, it was taken on the eve of the passing of the Law of Common and Free Schools in 1884 [4] in the last weeks of December 1883 and the first weeks of 1884 – not a very convenient time, as it was the summer holidays and Christmas and New Year's festivities. The rush was argued for on the need to count with precise information to guide educational policies, but the radicalization of the debate between Catholics and secular Republicans in the wake of the Law was probably part of the hurry. For the national authorities, the numbers were to produce an argument that would support the expansion of schooling and would allow a discussion of the nature of the nation's financial support to the provinces, which was very much at stake.

The organization of data collection followed the model of the 1869 National Census. One thousand, five hundred and sixty-one census-takers, mostly teachers, went to each home to register all children from 5 to 14 years old, including those in domestic service. While this was a marginal note, it nonetheless made it clear that all individuals counted, and had to be counted, in the Republic. The Census also sent questionnaires to schools that were to be responded to by school principals and teachers, which will be discussed below.

One of the problems faced by the School Census was the lack of personnel and of intermediate bureaucracies. The country was divided into four sections, and these sections into districts that followed the political divisions into provinces. The districts were under the command of school inspectors or teachers, still a largely unprofessional body.[5] The decree included the organization of local boards with the participation of common citizens, but their activity is not mentioned in later reports, and it seems very likely that they were not organized, not only because of the haste with which the census was performed.[6]

In terms of the production of educational data, the instructions to the census-takers are an interesting source, and evidence some concerns about the quality of the data they could collect (but not to the extent of training these pollsters). The surveyors were told the exact words with which they should introduce themselves; also, they had to read the official decree aloud and make it clear it was a civic duty to answer the questions. They were asked to keep an eye on the household to report if some of the answers did not correspond with what was observed. There were traces of what would later become codified as the psychosocial dimensions of the interview (Otero, 2006, p. 41). The decree established fines to non-respondents.

The questionnaire surveyed how many children were at each home and how many of them attended schools. Each census-taker had a 20-page notebook to write his/her notes, which could cover up to 100 children. The notebook had a template of a table that summarized the information collected at each home, in order to expedite data processing. The categories concerning students addressed male/female distinctions in relation to school attendance (yes/no), and levels of literacy: able to read and write/reads only/not able to read and write. The Census also reviewed whether there were orphans in the household, deaf-mute, blind, albino, or hunchback children. While strange to our current understandings, the latter classification speaks of the visibility gained by issues of disability in a school system that was based on normalizing populations (cf. Puiggrós, 1990).

In a separate notebook, the taker would have to write down detailed information: the full name of the respondee, place of birth, type of school s/he attended, if s/he was able to read and write or only read or neither, where s/he learned to do it (at home or at school), the name of the father, tutor or person in charge and the nationality of this person, the address where they lived, and whether this person was an orphan. This other information was more qualitative and thus difficult to categorize and, as it will be shown below, it was not reported later. However, their presence reveals some concerns of the administration about the behavior and control of the population of children. For example, the question of where the children learned to read and write, if at school or at home, was germane to a project that wanted to expand schools but also mobilize social energies and resources for the schooling crusade.

The categories say a great deal not only because of what they make explicit but also because of what they keep silent. A first comment can be made on the lack of questions about the race of children. In opposition to colonial classification of races, liberal statistics sought to avoid any distinctions of race and also of property that had been the main basis of earlier systems of categorization (Otero, 1998). The statisticians also adhered to a methodological minimalism that was in vogue at that time (Otero, 2006), and it was said that, due to *métissage*, racial categories did not say much about the many shades that were present in Latino American societies. Thus, they made it a principle to ask about individuals irrespective of their affiliation with race or their income. Social and moral philosophies were not supposed to influence numbers, which were considered as transparent and neutral representations of reality.

In relation to race, there were different situations that have to be acknowledged when analyzing this negligence of the racial issue. First, there were the aboriginal groups, neglected and – some say purposefully – silenced. But also, Otero reports that there were signs of resistance from these groups to be counted (at least until 1914), since they associated the Census with the levy for the army. On the other hand, there was a marked racism on the part of the state scientists who believed nothing was lost if aboriginal people were not included in the Census. Gabriel Carrasco, one of the leading statisticians of that period, on the occasion of a provincial Census (Santa Fe, 1887), said that while there were aboriginal tribes in the north, they were statistically irrelevant.

> The number of individuals that are part of [this group] is difficult to calculate, for lack of data, and on the other hand it is not important if known, not only because it is small but also because there is no statistical value in the man who does not produce or consume, having embraced the vegetative life of a wild man [salvaje]. (Carrasco, quoted by Otero, 2006, p. 346)

Second, the Afro-Argentinean population had a different demographic and political situation. It diminished considerably in those years; whereas in 1830 they represented 30% of the population in urban areas, a few decades later and because of interracial marriage, underreporting (for example in the case of *trigueños*, light Black skin), and emigration to other Latin American countries, this proportion was reduced significantly. However, by 1880 the Black population was still larger than some nationalities included in the Census (i.e. Scandinavian or Nordic countries).

Instead of race, the classification that emerged was that of nationals/foreigners, in a binary logic that was heavily charged (Otero, 2006). The question of populating the Pampas with immigrants was a central project for the Republican elite, which had in mind the Northern European, Protestant family, which they pictured as hardworking and austere. By the 1880s, it was clear that the immigrants who were arriving came from Southern Europe, with poor levels of literacy and a high degree of instability in their adaptation to the country (many of them returned to Europe less than five years after). There was political turmoil with the birth of the trade unions, and associations of national communities started to fight to have their schools and journals in their own languages. The official rhetoric became more nationalistic and exclusivist, and turned to the melting pot as a metaphor for the homogeneous nationalization that was to take place (cf. Díaz, 2003; Otero, 2006, among many others).

The melting pot was conceived as a whitening process, in which the non-white identities (Natives, Blacks, Mestizos) were to be suppressed either through the transplanting of a new, white population into the Pampas or through acculturation ('education'). Population categories contributed to this shift, and in the end the mixed races of the Argentinean inhabitants were effaced. In 1895, the same Gabriel Carrasco quoted before, by then superintendent of the Second National Census, said that: 'The racial question, so important in the USA, does not exist in Argentina, where its population will soon be completely unified in a new and beautiful white race, product of all the European nations fertilized in American soil' (quoted in Otero, 2006, p. 351). These categories, then, were as removed as they could be from being neutral, 'raw data' collecting. They organized the population into political classes that served a particular strategy for nation-building.

Nationalities, then, became relevant in this new Europeanized nation. Sex was privileged as a main distinction in a given population. The education of women was perceived as a necessity for the building of an enlightened citizenship since the independence from Spain. Claims for co-education were strong and the advancement of education was dependent on including girls (Morgade, 1987). Making girls visible was a way to push forward their education. As it will be seen in the reports, the most advanced districts in the expansion of attendance rates were also the ones that showed higher rates for the inclusion of girls.

The inquiry about orphans raises the question of the family, particularly of the legitimacy of birth and of social and political distinctions that were at play (Cosse, 2002). This was an old issue in Ibero-American countries (Lavrin, 1991), but the problem of the family became more relevant with the waves of immigrants that had been populating Argentina since the 1870s. Demographic changes brought by young males coming alone to work, in temporary jobs, led to an increased instability of household structures. For the Republican elite, sanctioning a legitimate form for the family was a problem of governing a population as much as it was a moral problem. Orphans were put together with disabled children, all confined to abnormal classes of people.

As for schooling and literacy items, it was clear, as Latzina had said in 1877, that school attendance did not guarantee being literate. The problems of measuring literacy rates seem not to have been explored as much as other dimensions. The intermittent nature of school attendance made it more likely that many children learned to read and not to write; but also placed the question of which kinds of experiences were included under the broad category of 'attends school' (Schoffield, 1968). The categorization of the population in three categories (unable to read or write/able to read/able to read and write) was taken from international examples such as the French Census (Furet & Ozouf, 1982; Graff, 1987), although the inquiries were based 'on answers to questions, rather on direct tests of literacy abilities' (Schoffield, 1968, p. 319). These discussions were not taken up by Latzina or by other commentators (cf. Díaz, 2003).

There were other questionnaires that were to be filled by all school teachers and principals. They also constitute an interesting source for understanding how the administration thought of schools and the kinds of practices and objects that were supposed to be counted.

The survey was different for each type of school: primary, secondary, normal, and private and religious schools. They were long questionnaires, including 40 items that had sometimes sub-items and opened up several possibilities. The items included were grouped around themes: type of school (6 questions), building facilities (8), furniture and materials (5), school personnel (9), students (6), and general issues (5). The amount of detail goes against the methodological minimalism embraced by the statisticians of the period. For example, in relation to students, the questions included the total enrolment, distinguishing sex, for the school and for each subject, the latter being almost impossible to track in a secondary school. Other questions included the following: numbers of teachers and students, religious affiliations, types of buildings, type of instructional materials available in schools (9 possibilities [7]), whether students paid fees (and how much), teachers' salaries, teachers' and students' nationalities, if the amount of furniture was enough for the students of the schools [8], inspectors' visits to the school, subjects taught (of a list of 28 possibilities), among many others.

Above all, the breadth of these items shows that what was considered as data in education was still uncertain, and had flexible boundaries. Why, for example, were students' fees to be included in a school census? What reliability would the information provided by the school owner have? How were teachers' salaries reported, and by whom? Why were the inspectors' visits to the school included in the Census, when there must have been official reports of them? In a relatively new system, these questions could contribute in various directions: they could provide information as in an audit, and they could also make the actors more aware of the norms and expectations of what should happen in schools. The visibilizing of the items organized a norm and also a practical repertoire of what principals and teachers were supposed to watch and keep record of in their daily practices.

Interpreting the Numbers: between the narrative of failure and an educational crusade

Less than one month after the administration of the Census, Latzina wrote a brief report to the President of the National Council on Education that summarized the preliminary results for the city of Buenos Aires (see Figure 1). It should be noted that the city had recently been turned into the nation's capital, and its boundaries were being redefined, but this fact is not mentioned. All his analysis was based on an assumption of stability: the population grows in a steady curve, the space is the same, and the proportions don't change.

The first paragraph informed the logistics of the Census: how many people participated, how much it cost, and an overview judgment of its efficiency. Latzina did not forget that he was part of a state bureaucracy that had to account for its workings; also, given his military training, it is very likely that he had a military report in mind when writing.

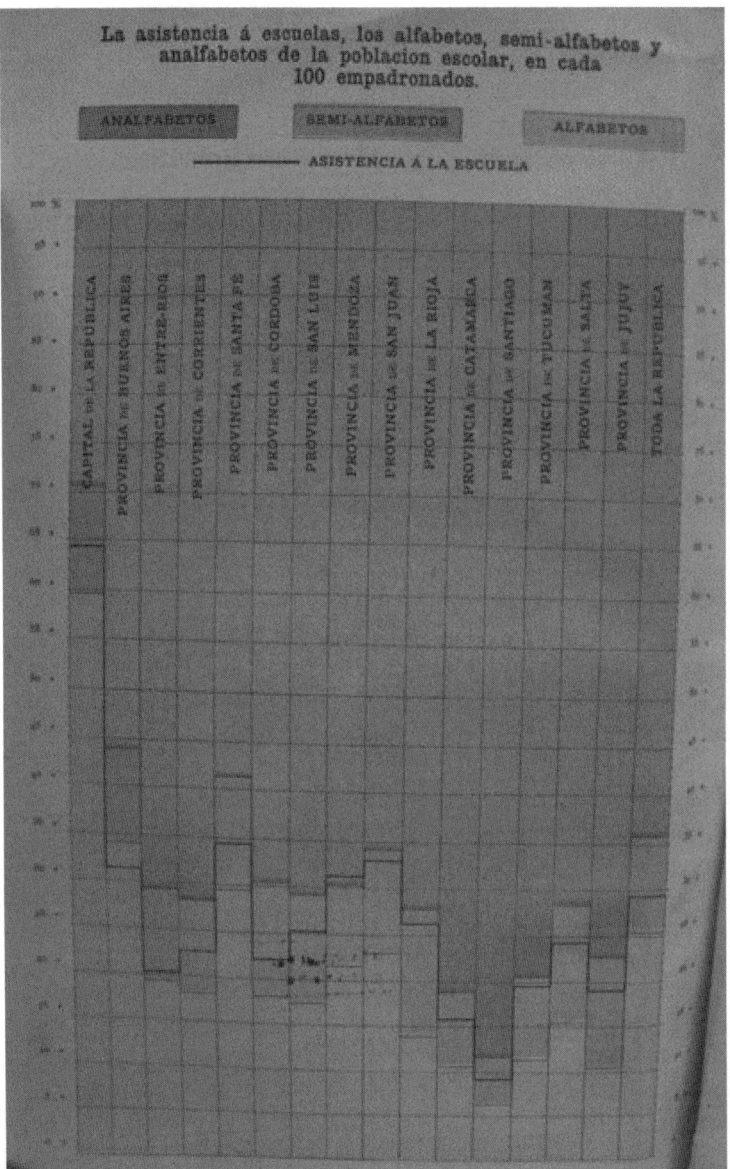

Figure 1. Resúmenes Generales en sumas absolutas y relativas del Censo Escolar Nacional levantado a fines de 1883 y principios de 1884 (General Briefings in absolute and relative sums of the National School Census taken at the end of 1883 and beginning of 1884). Buenos Aires: Stiller & Laass (1884).

109

As for the results themselves, Latzina stated that the population between 5 and 14 years old in the city was of 51,785 children, of which 33,822 attended schools – a proportion he finds 'unflattering' (Latzina, 1884a, p. 424). In the last group, girls slightly outnumbered boys: 17,058 versus 16,734 (p. 425). Those who could read and write totaled 30,959 (again, girls had a small advantage over boys), and those who could only read were 5793 children (more boys than girls). This early inclusion of females in elementary schools was not analyzed or valued in his briefing. The narrative style is dry and somewhat dull, and there are only a few paragraphs in which he uses adjectives. Latzina also reported on other population categories: the Census counted 1727 orphans ('either because their parents died, or they are illegitimate children abandoned by their mother or father', p. 424), 48 deaf-mute, 31 blind, 40 albino, and 39 hunchback. The small quantities of these groups make it even more explicit to what extent these were theoretical categories applied to the population; as in the case of the Afro-Argentineans against the Scandinavian immigrants, there were groups that had to be visibilized, while others (aboriginal groups, internal migrants, Blacks) were not to be counted.

Latzina performed some operations with the figures that also show the 'leap of faith' asked by statisticians. First, due to the lack of a population census with which he could compare the numbers of the School Census (the only general Census had been taken in 1869, 14 years before), he projected a probabilistic calculus based on keeping stable the percentage of children aged 5-14 years old over the general population in 1869 and 1883-84 (which happened to be 18.2%), which led him to conclude that the city should have 283,758 inhabitants in 1883. But he also added the individuals who could be traveling or outside the city because of holidays, which would amount to 16,000 (he does not explain how he gets this number). It is not clear why he needed to calculate the general population to report about schools (in fact, the Census surveys all children in families, not only those who go to school), but he used two pages to explain his reasoning. The 'informed guessing' seems to be part of the argument of the statistician: 'I am inclined to believe that this numeral is not far from the truth'[9] (Latzina, 1884a, p. 423).

Second, Latzina presented the information distinguishing boys and girls, and also the 14 parishes of the city. Sex and geographic distribution were the privileged variables that organized data. In relation to what was said in the past section, while sex was presumably a central category, evident in the organization of charts by surveyors, the geographic distribution could only come after local data collection and after constructing a panoramic view. The stress that Latzina put on this variable probably reinforced this privileged position of seeing from above and comparing, something that could only be done at the central level.

One and a half months later, Latzina wrote another report including the preliminary findings for four western and northern provinces of the country (San Luis, San Juan, Catamarca and Tucumán). Latzina had lived in

Catamarca so he would have known the singularities of the region. He also began assessing the performance of the team, the costs and the efficiency of the operation – as a field marshal. But the report differs from the previous one in tone and narrative. The findings, which showed the low expansion of schooling away from the littoral provinces, were discouraging for the statistician or, better said, for the statesman. In these provinces, less than a quarter of the children between 5 and 14 years old attended schooling; of this, boys surpassed girls by almost 8 points. The percentage of children who could read and write was 10.5% in Catamarca and 11.6% in Tucumán; San Juan performed slightly better, with 23.5%. Latzina also reported on the internal inequalities in each province: considering the differences among parishes, the literacy rates showed variations of 5 or 6 times between the lowest and the highest. Illiteracy rates were too high for a 'country ruled by democratic principles': Tucumán had 79.4% of illiterates among children, while San Juan, the lowest in the group, had 66.1%. In San Juan, in a rural district (La Huerta), no children knew how to read and/or write; Latzina denounced the 'complete and absolute absence of an intellectual culture' that 'victimizes the children of this district' (Latzina, 1884b, p. 592). The language of description gave way to the language of interpretation; this report is charged with denunciations inscribed in a 'politics of pity' toward poor children who were presented as victims of society (Boltanski, 1991).

The report included a retrospective overview, which compared the findings of 1869 and 1883 for the children aged between 5 and 14. The comparison was more careful than in the previous report, as he contrasted the same population group and did not make any 'informed guess' about the general population. He characterized the changes as 'a barely noticeable progress': he noted only small increases in the school attendance rates (better in San Luis, from 15.2% to 25.4%, than in Catamarca, from 13.5% to 15.7%), and even a decrease in San Juan (from 33.6% to 32.8%) (Latzina, 1884b, p. 593). However, not for a moment did he doubt the technique for collecting data, or provide other information about the province that might have helped to conceptualize these slight gains or decreases.

Concluding Remarks

Latzina provides a good example of the scientists-intellectuals that were central to the institutional and epistemological production of educational data in the nineteenth century. Located in an international network of languages and authorities, and an immigrant himself, he contributed to the construction of a machinery of the state that was set to count, classify and compare the population. It helped build a centralized knowledge that could put together disparate pieces, translate local cases into homogeneous categories, and thus produce an image of the country from above that diagnosed a state of affairs and located each element in a hierarchy. The idea of a white, European, literate nation was central to this process of counting and describing the population, and this idea marginalized and invisibilized ample segments of Argentineans.

Latzina combined technical expertise with the will of the politician, and was not shy at interpreting what he saw in the educational situation. He concluded that the efforts to advance elementary education were a big failure – an interpretation that was quite useful for the Republican elite to promote the passing of a new law and reorganize power relations between local governments and national authorities. The description of a catastrophic situation, particularly in the northern provinces, gave strong legitimacy to the intervention of the national state. 'Raw data' was mobilized within narratives that were inscribed into a politics of pity and indignation, and that were helpful in rallying support for specific policies.

There are, of course, other sides to this story, and many other ways of telling it. Luc Boltanski and Laurent Thévenot (2006) insist that any regime of justification is never total or complete. The magic of numbers was not a spell that worked on everybody, nor did it work steadily. The Vice-Consul of Argentina in Spain wrote in 1887, while stationed in Las Palmas (Canary Islands), that 'nothing is more useful than the study of general statistics of elementary schooling for getting to know the march of instruction in advanced countries ... . However, the numbers provided by the Census do not have for the subscriber but a relative value, for the simple reason that in the [Argentine] Republic an average of 45,566 individuals immigrate yearly in times of peace' (Díaz Aguilar, 1887, p. 684). Educational statistics never reigned unquestioned in Argentina and, for multiple reasons, it was frequently shunned by other legitimating rhetorics. But the episodes presented in this chapter show the need to continue problematizing what counts as educational data, and reflect on what was left aside.

Notes

[1] As Mary Poovey (1998, p. xix) says, 'all systematic knowledge systems require something like a leap of faith' because they are based on abstractions or theoretical abstractions which cannot be observed (mind, market, population).

[2] A separation that refers not only to the realm of research and philosophy, but also to that of painting and mapping. See Alpers (1983).

[3] President Domingo F. Sarmiento (1811-88) played an important role in the hiring of these scientific cadres in the late 1860s and early 1870s, and these foreigners were central to the first scientific museum in Buenos Aires (1861, Karl Konrad Burmeister), the first Military School (1869, Janos Cztez), the Astronomical Observatory in Córdoba (1870, Benjamin Gould), among other institutional creations.

[4] The 1420 Law has been equated to the Ferry Laws in France, and established a common school, tuition-free and secular (religion was to be taught after hours).

[5] Normal Schools had been created in the early 1870s. There were just a few school inspectors, as it will be seen in the next section.

[6] Cf. Lucila Minvielle's doctoral dissertation on the failure of local educational boards at that time (2009).

[7] These were mural blackboards, rules and compasses; wall maps; world globes and astronomical globes; collection of solids (stones and others) and geometry sets; wall charts of natural history; laboratories for physics, chemistry and mechanics; models (cast or lithographies) for drawing; and math sets for lineal drawing. Note that no mention is made of textbooks or notebooks.

[8] This question visibly appeals to a personal opinion or impression by the respondent, and did not involve numbers.

[9] 'Me inclino a creer, que este guarismo dista muy poco de la verdad.'

References

Alpers, S. (1983) The Art of Describing. Dutch Art in the Seventeenth Century. Chicago: Chicago University Press.

Boltanski, L. (1991) Distant Suffering. Morality, Media and Politics. Cambridge: Cambridge University Press.

Boltanski, L. & Thévenot, L. (2006) On Justification. Economies of Worth, trans. Catherine Porter. Princeton, NJ: Princeton University Press.

Censo Escolar correspondiente a fines de 1883 y principios de 1884. Levantado bajo la superintendencia administrativa de la Comisión Nacional de Educación, compuesta por el Dr. Benjamin Zorrilla y compilado bajo la dirección de Francisco Latzina, Jefe de la Oficina Central del Censo. Buenos Aires: Talleres de la Tribuna Nacional, 1885.

Cosse, I. (2002) Estigmas de nacimiento en una época de justicia y ascenso social. Filiación ilegítima y familia (1946-1954). Master's thesis, Universidad de San Andrés, Argentina.

Daston, L. (1991) Baconian Facts, Academic Civility, and the Prehistory of Objectivity, Annals of Scholarship, 8(3-4), 337-364.

Daston, L. & Galison, P. (2007) Objectivity. New York: Zone Books.

David, J. (2003) Régimes descriptifs du XIXe siècle. Le typique et le pittoresque dans l'enquête et le roman, in G. Blundo & J.-P. Olivier de Sardan (Eds) Pratiques de la description, pp. 185-210. Paris: Éditions de l'École des hautes études en sciences sociales.

De La Peña, S. & Wilkie, J. (1994) La estadística económica en México. Los orígenes. México DF: Siglo XXI editores.

DePaepe, M. (1992) Experimental Research in Education 1890-1940: historical processes behind the development of a discipline in Western Europe and the United States, in M. Whitehead (Ed.) Education and Europe: historical and contemporary Perspectives, pp. 67-93. Hull: Studies in Education.

Desrosières, A. (1999) The History of Statistics as a Genre: styles of writing and social uses, paper presented at the conference 'Statistical Internationalism, State

Practices, and National Traditions: progress report and prospects in the history of statistics', University of Quebec, 22-23 September.

Díaz, B. (2003) La prescripción de la pericia educativa. Un estudio metafórico sobre la conformación de la estadística educativa en la Argentina de fines del siglo XIX y principios del siglo XX. Buenos Aires, Tesis de Maestría en Ciencias Sociales con orientación en Educación, FLACSO/Argentina.

Díaz Aguilar, C. (1887) Nota a Su Excelencia el señor Ministerio de Relaciones Exteriores, El Monitor de la Educación Común, 8(118), 683-686.

Dodier N. (1996) Les sciences sociales face à la raison statistique (note critique), Annales. Histoire, Sciences Sociales, 51(2), 409-428.

Furet, F. & Ozouf, J. (1982) Reading and Writing: literacy in France from Calvin to Jules Ferry. Cambridge: Cambridge University Press.

Graff, H. (1987) The Legacies of Literacy. Continuities and Contradictions in Western Culture and Society. Bloomington: Indiana University Press.

Hacking, I. (1995) The Looping Effects of Human Kinds, in D. Sperber, D. Premack & A. Premack (Eds) *Causal Cognition. An Interdisciplinary Approach*, pp. 351-383. Oxford: Oxford University Press.

Larsen, M. (2004) Counting, Classifying and Comparing: contemporary policies and practices to govern and control the 21st century teacher, paper delivered at the 21st Comparative Education Society in Europe (CESE) conference, Copenhagen, June.

Latour, B. (2005) Reassembling the Social. An Introduction to Actor–Network Theory. Oxford: Oxford University Press.

Latzina, F. (1884a) Censo Escolar de la Capital, El Monitor de la Educación Común, 3(53), 423-426.

Latzina, F. (1884b) Resultados generales y preliminares del Censo Escolar, El Monitor de la Educación Común, 3(59), 590-593.

Latzina, F. (1885) Virutas y astillas. Informe sobre el estado de las escuelas primarias y secundarias en las provincias de Córdoba, Corrientes, Entre Ríos y Santa Fe. Buenos Aires: Edición Litográfica Imprenta y Encuadernación de Estillar y Laass.

Latzina, F. (1914) Tercer Censo Nacional, Tomo IV. Buenos Aires: Talleres Gráficos de L.J. Rosso y Cía.

Lavrin, A. (Ed.) (1991) Sexualidad y matrimonio en la América hispánica. Siglos XVI-XVIII. México DF: Grijalbo-CONACULTA.

Mercante, V. (1918) La crisis de la pubertad. Buenos Aires: Cabaut.

Minvielle, L. (2009) El gobierno local de la educación en la provincia de Buenos Aires a fines del Siglo XIX: ¿crónica de una muerte anunciada? Doctoral dissertation, Escuela de Educación, Universidad de San Andrés, Argentina.

Morgade, G. (Ed.) (1987) Mujeres en la educación. Género y docencia en la Argentina, 1870-1930. Buenos Aires: Miño y Dávila editores.

Otero, H. (1998) Estadística censal y construcción de la nación. El caso argentino, 1869-1914, Boletín del Instituto de Historia Argentina y Americana Dr. Emilio Ravignani, nos. 16-17, 123-149.

Otero, H. (2006) Estadística y nación. Una historia conceptual del pensamiento censal de la Argentina moderna, 1869-1914. Buenos Aires: Prometeo Libros.

Poovey, M. (1998) A History of the Modern Fact. Problems of Knowledge in the Sciences of Wealth and Society. Chicago: Chicago University Press.

Puiggrós, A. (1990) Sujetos, disciplina y curriculum en los orígenes del sistema educativo argentino (1885-1916). Buenos Aires: Galerna.

Schoffield, R.S. (1968) The Measurement of Literacy in Pre-Industrial England, in J. Goody (Ed.) Literacy in Traditional Societies, pp. 311-325. Cambridge: Cambridge University Press.

Visualising Girls' Secondary Education in Interwar Europe: Amélie Arató's *L'Enseignement secondaire des jeunes filles en Europe*

JOYCE GOODMAN

SUMMARY This chapter examines the diagrams of education systems in Amélie Arató's study of girls' secondary education, published in 1934 as *L'Enseignement secondaire des jeunes filles en Europe*. The author begins by tracing the strategies Arató employed to organise the comparative data in her account. She locates Arató's use of visual representation in the context of the rise of educational and information sciences and their link to the practices of interwar cooperative internationalism at the International Bureau of Education in Geneva, which Arató visited in 1931 during the course of her research. The chapter concludes by discussing the contradictions inherent in Arató's use of visualisations in a project to 'progress' education for women and girls; and the author concludes by pointing to the complexities of international comparative data for policy purposes in education.

Introduction

In 1934, the Hungarian Amélie Arató published *L'Enseignement secondaire des jeunes filles en Europe* (Arató, 1934). This was the outcome of two years' research into girls' secondary education in Europe and America commissioned by the International Federation of University Women (IFUW) as part of their agenda to internationalise learning and knowledge and to promote university women's careers (Goodman, 2011). Arató's *L'Enseignement secondaire des jeunes filles en Europe* (see Figure 1) added to the small number of comparative studies of girls' secondary education published from the late 1890s onwards as a small but growing international feminist movement shared information on other school systems in order to challenge national stereotypes regarding women's more fragile minds or constitutions

117

(Rogers, 2006; Albisetti et al, 2010, pp. 1-8).[1] Each study provided a 'slow accretion of layers of sophistication' (Phillips & Schweisfurth, 2007, p. 38) in comparative accounts of education for women and girls. What stood out in Arató's study was the systematic use of the diagrams of education systems for the 26 countries she visited. These illustrated the position of girls' schooling and provided a transportable, transnational methodology amenable to reading across borders, irrespective of written language proficiency (Livingstone, 2005).[2]

Figure 1. Amélie Arató, *L'Enseignement secondaire des jeunes filles en Europe* (Arató, 1934, frontispiece).

During the course of her research Arató visited the International Bureau of Education (IBE) in Geneva. When Arató arrived at the IBE in 1931 (IBE, 1931e, p. 91), Elsie Schatzmann was working on the diagrams of education systems incorporated in *L'Organisation de l'instruction publique dans 53 pays*, jointly published with Albin Jakiel in 1933 (IBE, 1933), which Arató referenced in her account. These 61 diagrams of education systems reflected the IBE's interest in forms through which knowledge was represented and disseminated. This systematic use of diagrams illustrates a link from the IBE to the rise of information sciences in Europe (Boyd Rayward, 2008, p. 16). Like educational sciences, information sciences formed part of interwar cooperative internationalism that saw the discovery of empirical facts and their rational application as a means of promoting inter- and intra-societal cooperation by replacing the dominant state-interest perspective of international relations with a knowledge-based one (Fritz, 2005, pp. 142-144).

In this chapter I aim to 'wrest' the diagrams of education systems that form Arató's visual technologies out of a teleological history of the rise of comparative educational data on education for girls and women, by placing them alongside other cultural currents from which they emerged (Savage, 2010, p. 238). I begin by locating Arató as a researcher in terms of expertise and by outlining the strategies she used to organise the data in her account. In the second section I provide a broader context for Arató's systematic use of diagrams by focusing on visualisation techniques within processes of documentalism and the scientisation of knowledge as elements in practices of interwar cooperative internationalism at the IBE. Here I follow Popkewitz, who argues that various sciences overlap in the system of reason that gives intelligibility to science as a practice of planning (Popkewitz, 2005, p. 4). In the concluding section, I discuss contradictions inherent in Arató's diagrams of educational systems in terms of the project to transport knowledge of advances in girls' education across international borders and to 'progress' education for women and girls. Here I draw on Mike Savage's appropriation of Latour's actor–network theory in emphasising the agency of inscription, technical devices and mundane instruments used in research activity that social groups are mobilised by and themselves deploy (Savage, 2010, p. 12).

Organising Data on Girls' Secondary Education in Europe

The university-educated women of the IFUW commissioned Arató for their study on the basis of her expertise with educational questions, knowledge of French, English, German and Italian, Spanish or a Slav language, and availability to devote two years to the research (IFUW, 1930, p. 40; Little, 1932, p. 81).[3] Arató's 'expert' status reflected developments in Hungarian social science as well as the increasing professionalisation of teachers in Hungary and the place of women in both developments (Nemeth, 2006, p. 170).[4]

As a professional expert, Arató's aim was to use social research in a framework of social reform to illustrate the challenge for contemporary women of the best means to create the most appropriate education to fulfil the ambitions of the 'modern woman' (Arató, 1934, p. 29). Having observed a range of systems, processes, practices and experiences during her two years spent researching (pp. 7-8), Arató's task was to produce a text that would satisfy the IFUW's requirement to be systematic; for her commission had resulted from an earlier 1925 IFUW investigation into national systems of secondary schooling for girls, the position of women teachers within them and the extent of girls' curricula, which had provided a series of broad headlines but had raised questions of data equivalence given the different meanings of secondary education held in different countries (IFUW, 1925, p. 43).[5] To deal with problems of terminology around secondary education, which, in some countries, designated a stage of education between primary school and university, while in others it denoted schools which were preparing pupils exclusively for university studies, Arató excluded from her research professional schools and the *écoles supérieures de jeunes filles* (Arató, 1934, p. 30).

Arató researched girls' education in England, Germany, Austria, Belgium, Bulgaria, Denmark, Estonia, Finland, France, Greece, Holland, Hungary, Ireland, Italy, Latvia, Lithuania, Luxemburg, Norway, Poland, Romania, Russia, Sweden, Switzerland, Czechoslovakia, Yugoslavia and the United States. To illustrate the contemporary challenges of education for the 'modern woman' (p. 29), she constructed the majority of her text with a forward focus. But she opened with an historical account that located this part of her study in the historical-philosophical tradition of comparativists like Michael Sadler and Isaac Kandel. Here, she charted a narrative of decline from a golden age for women that feminist writers employed to demonstrate that intellectual power was independent of sex (p. 11), leading to the position in the nineteenth century, when the growth of secondary education had led women to the 'doors' of the university. She painted the nineteenth century as a time of prejudice, with barriers overturned only by changes in the economic fortunes that had led European universities to open their doors to a new type of young woman, prepared for all eventualities and ready to play her full part in life (p. 16).

In her study of contemporary education, Arató approached her task thematically and at times drew on personal observation (p. 80). In other places she took readers through conclusions based on international comparison (p. 90). She warmed to the Dalton Plan in Holland, England, Germany, Australia and Finland (p. 189), was critical of ways in which 'traditional' secondary education was organised (p. 99), and condemned the influence of examinations (p. 190). Nonetheless, she structured sections of *L'Enseignement secondaire des jeunes filles en Europe* around notions of 'liberal' education, with chapters on intellectual, moral and physical education. The chapter on intellectual education covered hours of schooling, curricula, examinations and organisation of lessons; the physical education chapter included health and hygiene; while the moral education chapter discussed coeducation and the preparation of girls for their future roles in society. Other chapters discussed educational structures, administration, organisation, and types of secondary schools; the position of women in education, including teacher training; women teachers; women head teachers; women inspectors; and the position of women in educational administration.

Arató's analysis of contemporary education in *L'Enseignement secondaire des jeunes filles en Europe* fell into two distinct parts. Part 1 included diagrams of the education systems of countries she visited. She identified six models of stratified education systems and outlined the national organisation and position of girls and boys within the systems (single sex or coeducation). She identified these as:

1. Le système des types séparés;
2. Le système de la bifurcation;
3. Le système mixte (type et bifurcation);
4. Le système parallèle;
5. Le système traditionnel;
6. L'école secondaire unique (p. 30).

Each country was represented systematically as in the exemplar diagrams (Figures 2, 3 and 4).

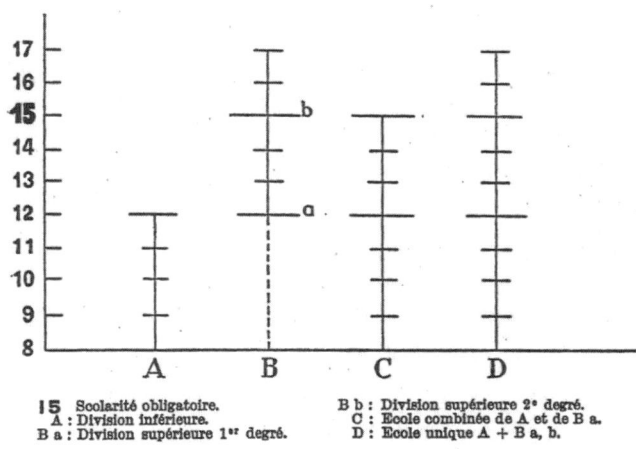

Figure 2. L'école secondaire unique: Union des républiques socialistes soviétiques (Arató, 1934, p. 64).

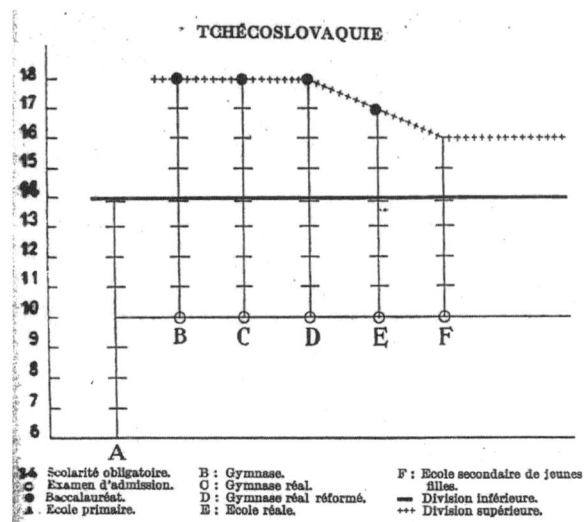

Figure 3. Le système des types séparés: Tchécoslovaquie (Arató, 1934, p. 39).

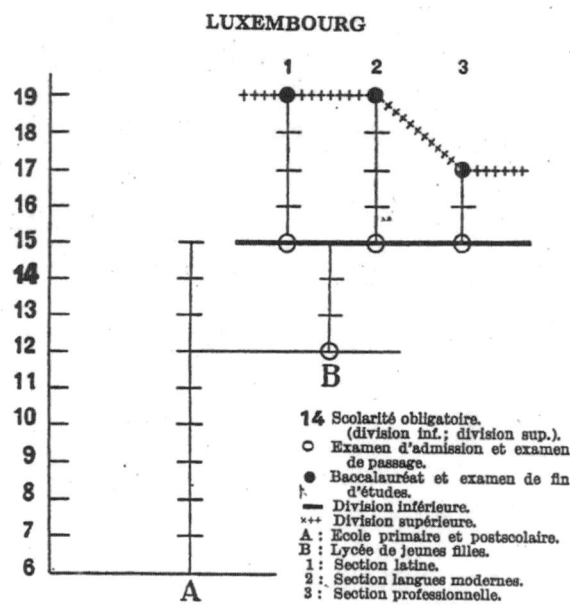

Figure 4. Le système de la bifurcation: Luxembourg (Arató, 1934, p. 49).

In the thematic chapters of Part 2 dealing with the position of women, Arató organised discussion of the data largely through alphabetical ordering of countries, although she also grouped together countries to make specific points. Part 2 included the type of descriptive statistics that had become the stock in trade of comparative educationists from the days of Victor Cousin onwards (Goodman, 2002). When discussing the curriculum, she drew up tables of hours devoted to each curriculum subject for a range of countries organised alphabetically by country. These included many instances of a curriculum for girls that she described as specifically feminine (Arató, 1934, pp. 110-112, 114-116, 138-147, 150-165). In the chapter devoted to the preparation of girls for their future role, when presenting information by country alphabetically, she drew together conclusions for the reader (pp. 225-228). Where examples from her observations, discussions with teachers, and texts that she encountered on her travels struck her as particularly interesting she departed from these practices. In a section on coeducation, for example, she drew on data from a text by Agnes Molton, who had undertaken an enquiry in a boarding school in Germany (*Aufbauschule*) where pupils of both sexes had been asked to write an essay on coeducation (pp. 195-196).

The alphabetical ordering of data resulted in Arató shaping the majority of Part 2 of *L'Enseignement secondaire des jeunes filles en Europe* around ideological common sense, territorial notions of national borders and territory as the basis of international comparison (Goodman, 2011). In countries where she found national identities most marked, as in England (Arató, 1934, p. 207) and Italy (pp. 205-206), she discussed national particularities and sought to understand phenomena in terms of the relation between education and national characteristics. This aligned with the importance placed on understanding national context in the work of comparativists like Sadler and Kandel (Kandel, 1933, p. 23). By the time Arató was conducting her research, notions of national self-determination advanced by the League of Nations had led to the re-alignment of national borders and the creation of new nation states across Europe (Sluga, 2006, chapter 2). As a result many new states artificially encompassed disparate nationalities in the wake of the Treaty of Versailles that were in tension with contemporary notions of national self-determination (Hupchick & Cox, 2001, map 42). Despite the territorial notions of borders through which her text was organised, in Part 1 of *L'Enseignement secondaire des jeunes filles en Europe* Arató provided statistical data to chart national minorities and languages and how these related to schooling. For example, the statistical data in her account for national minorities and languages in Lithuania and Latvia (Arató, 1934, pp. 68-73) played into linguistic-cultural conceptions of nation (Wendland, 2011, pp. 407, 441)[6] and demonstrated the inchoateness and non-fixity of national meanings and identifications in the interwar period around the interpenetration of *nation* and *citizenry* (Eley, 2000, pp. 28, 30).[7]

In the following section I look in more detail at Arató's systematic use in Part 1 of her text of diagrams of education systems, by discussing the relationship between the development of research, information sciences and documentalism at the IBE in Geneva, which Arató visited in 1931 during the course of her research (IBE, 1931e, p. 91).

Research, Information Sciences, Documentalism and Data Visualisation at the International Bureau of Education in Geneva

At the point when Arató visited the IBE, Elsie Schatzmann was working on the diagrams published in *L'Organisation de l'instruction publique dans 53 pays* (IBE, 1933) (see Figure 5). Like Albin Jackiel, with whom the text was published, Schatzmann was a member of the IBE's section of School Organisation and Legislation, which formed part of the Research Division of the IBE (p. iv). When Robert Dottrens presented the report of the Council on the Reorganisation of the Constitution to the IBE Assembly in 1929, he spoke of the IBE as a place for the international organisation of documentation and information as well as a place for research. These three aspects were reflected in the organisation of the IBE into divisions, each made up of several sections (IBE, 1929b, pp. 3, 7).

The IBE's Research Division was charged with inquiries and technical studies. It aimed 'by scientific and objective methods to find out the degree of success of measures, both theoretical and practical, taken throughout the world in the sphere of education' (IBE, 1930a, p. 8). The Research Division was originally organised into sections dealing with physical education, intellectual education, moral education, international education, parent education, rural education, school organisation and legislation, and child psychology. In the area of school organisation and legislation, the work of the Research Division resonated with the work of the Information Division. The Information Division aimed to centralise documents relating to education and organise the exchange of information. The division reviewed books and periodicals from different countries and classified the information for use in IBE publications and for the information of visitors. It prepared articles on important educational events and on the work of the IBE; replied to requests for information from governments and national and international education organisations and institutions; and kept in touch with national correspondents. The division was charged with the translation, editing and distribution of the IBE *Bulletin* and the IBE's other publications (and eventually *The Yearbook*), the library and exhibitions. It was originally organised in six sections, comprising documentation, information, publication, statistics, propaganda, and national correspondents (IBE, 1930a, p. 8).

Figure 5. L'Organisation de l'instruction publique dans 53 pays
(IBE, 1933, frontispiece).

Between the wars the IBE's Information Division engaged in activities that Boyd Rayward (2008) identified as key interests of documentalists. The IBE produced bibliographies and, to 'facilitate the classing in a card-index of the educational news and book reviews', the division worked on the classification of educational documents prefixing each item with its decimal classification number and a subject heading (Rossello, 1944, p. 15). This system was eventually published as the *Plan for the Classification of Educational Documents* (IBE, n.d.). The IBE also moved away from previous ledger-based systems by introducing card indexes, which, Boyd Rayward notes, incorporated

Taylorist and Fordist ideas but also formal modes of representation (classification numbers, for example) and standardisation of information (Boyd Rayward, 2008, p. 12). In order that its information service would be carried out as efficiently as possible, the IBE continually added to its library of scientific and practical educational works, school legislation, books on child psychology, educational periodicals (before the war about 500 periodicals in many different languages were received regularly), adding particularly important subjects to its card index of educational information and to its selected bibliographies in English and French (Rossello, 1933, p. 115).

Information collection, information management and information sharing about education, alongside initiation of scientific investigations and statistical enquiries (Rossello, 1944, p. 116), formed part of the IBE's agenda around intellectual cooperation in the pursuit of peace. Within a framework of cooperative internationalism, these activities constituted overlapping practices that gave 'intelligibility to science as a practice of planning' and 'intelligibility to the possibilities of thought and action' (Popkewitz, 2006, pp. 162, 163).[8] The IBE's 1929 Constitution noted that the development of education was an 'essential factor in the establishment of peace and in the moral and material progress of humanity' (Rossello, 1944, p. 116) and that, in order to promote this development, it was important to collect educational data to facilitate the exchange of information so that each country could profit by the experience of others (p. 116). Information and research were to be organised according to a strictly scientific and objective spirit which, the IBE maintained, placed it in a neutral position with regard to national, political and religious questions. The notion of objective yet reformist science in which knowledge and the interdependence of countries were seen as 'two sides of the same coin' characterised the rhetoric of cooperative internationalism at the League of Nations (Fritz, 2005, pp. 142-144), where belief in the ability of the 'expert' to create the spirit of internationalism through 'the provision of "scientized", "disinterested", "objective" knowledge underpinned notions of the "intellectual"' (Goodman, 2011, p. 718).[9]

The links from the IBE to the Union of International Associations at Brussels were important to the IBE's developing use of graphic visualisation of data. The Union was directed by Henri La Fontaine, who occupied the chair of international law at the Free University of Brussels, and Paul Otlet, the documentalist and internationalist (Rossello, 1944, p. 51; Boyd Rayward, 2008, p. 11). In 1895, La Fontaine and Otlet had called an international conference to consider the creation of a universal catalogue for everything that had been published, 'a repertory which would allow mobilisation of and access to knowledge in a new, globally-based way' (Boyd Rayward, 2008, p. 13). The result was the establishment of the Institut international de bibliographie, which led in 1910 to the foundation of the Union of International Associations. To this was added an international museum, at what was called first the Palais Mondial and later the Mundaneum. Here a universal bibliographical catalogue on cards was developed, which contained 16 million entries by 1930, and Otlet followed his interests in knowledge representation, especially its visual forms (Boyd Rayward, 2008, pp. 14,16).

In 1927-28, in conjunction with Otlet and his co-worker Anne Oderfeld, the General Assembly of the IBE established a committee to study the question of International Didactic Material. The aim was to develop an *Atlas de la civilisation universelle*, which they termed the *Nuovo Orbis Pictus*, referring back to the visualisations in the *Orbis Pictus* by Comenius. The aim of the *Atlas* was to present each territory, people and culture in tabular fashion to support the teaching of international peace. The images in the *Atlas* were to be published on separate sheets of engraving so that maps, graphs, etc. could be combined in various ways, and attached to university decimal classifications (Van den Heuvel, 2008, pp. 134, 135). The question of the teaching materials was put on the agenda of the 1929 IBE conference and displayed in the conference exhibition (IBE, 1929a, p. 2), and a report of the joint committee was later published (Otlet & Oderfeld, 1929). The *Atlas* was not to progress with the IBE but would be picked up again by Otlet with Otto Neurath, a promoter of visual statistics (Hartmann, 2008, pp. 279-294; Nikolow, 2008, pp. 257-258), although it would not be completed.

Concurrent with the discussions about the *Atlas* with Otlet and Oderfeld, Schatzmann was preparing *L'Organisation de l'instruction publique dans 53 pays* for publication. In his report to the IBE Council in 1929, retiring IBE director Pierre Bovet noted that Schatzmann's work on the organisation of public education in 50 different countries was being interpreted 'by a magnificent collection of diagrams'. He reported that these formed a feature of the IBE stand at the exhibition organised in connection with the conference at Geneva at which representatives of ministries of education were to be present (IBE, 1929b, p. 2).

Work on *L'Organisation de l'instruction publique dans 53 pays* was begun by the IBE section of School Organisation and Legislation, collating and abstracting all the official documents that had been published previously and presenting the data in tables and graphs. The diagrams (showing infant, primary, secondary, higher and professional education) with commentary formed one of four elements that were to be published for each country. The diagrams were to be complemented with information about examinations and their connections to parts of the system, statistics and a bibliography; and were to be preceded by preliminary information on population, number of children of school age, percentage in schooling, and the ages of compulsory schooling (IBE, 1933, p. v).[10] While the publication was to be a working tool, rather than simply a collection of facts, the aim was to present an enumeration that was as complete as possible (p. v) (see Figure 6).

To facilitate comparison of the organisation of schooling in different countries, some parts of the education 'system' were excluded. Only a general framework was presented (numbers of degrees, length of studies, relationship between different types of schools) and no attempt was made to represent the internal organisation of the school, or methods and programmes.

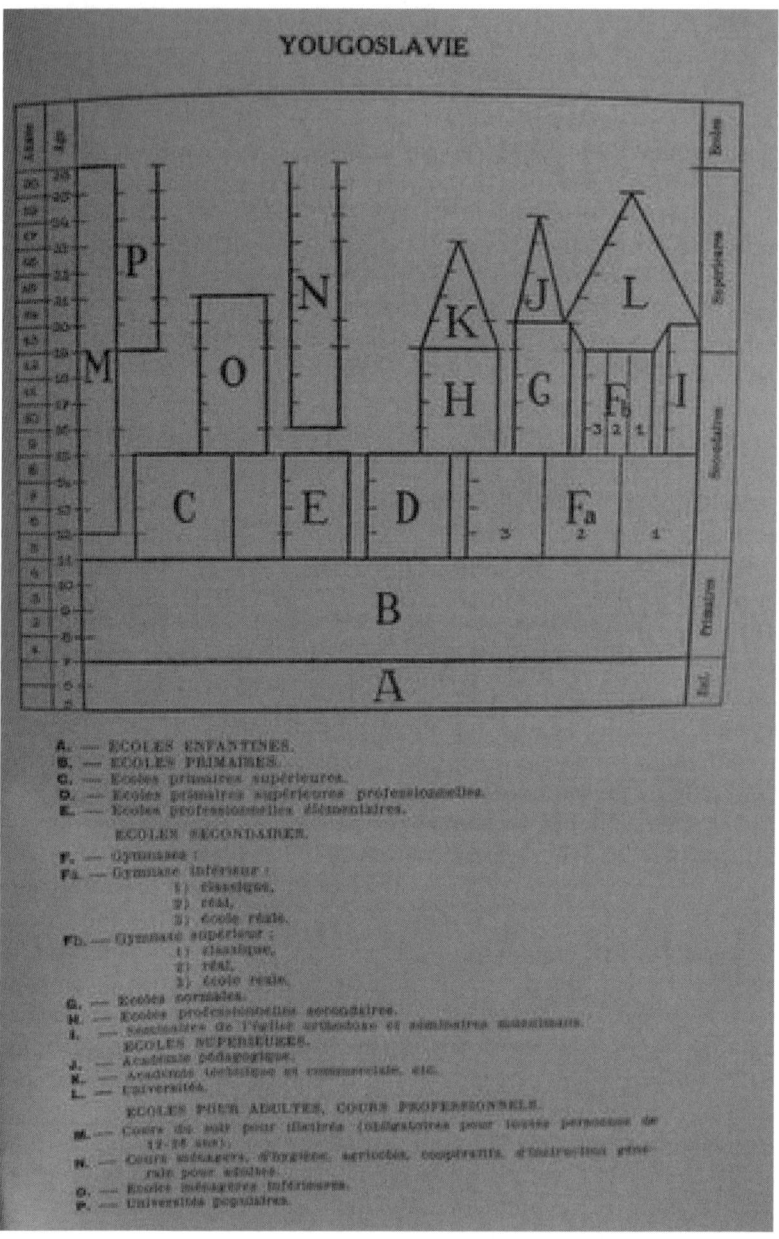

Figure 6. 'Yougoslavie' (IBE, 1933, p.367).

Only official information from ministries was included and only information on state-maintained schooling. Private schools were to be excluded (despite the fact that they were more numerous and in some places identical to those of the state), as well as special schools for children with disabilities. The difficulty of detailing the complexity of professional schools in different countries was also recognised (p. vii). In 1930 and 1931, the IBE *Bulletin* reported that data collected so far for *L'Organisation de l'instruction publique dans 53 pays* was being sent to the various ministries for revision and that work was progressing on the elaboration of the diagrams (IBE, 1930b, p. 6; 1931a, p. 4, 1931c, p. 44; 1931d, p. 90). Following the return of corrected information the diagrams were then rebuilt and reviewed by ministries (IBE, 1933, p. 7) and the final diagrams drawn for publication by M. le docteur Heller (p. viii). From 1931 *L'Organisation de l'instruction publique dans 53 pays* was being advertised at a pre-publication price of 10 francs (IBE, 1931b, p. 6) prior to publication.

When it was published, *L'Organisation de l'instruction publique dans 53 pays* was cited by Arató in the bibliography of *L'Enseignement secondaire des jeunes filles en Europe*. Isaac Kandel, now at the International Institute, Teachers College Columbia, also cited it in his 1933 *Comparative Education* (Kandel, 1933). Graphic representation of education systems was not new in Teachers College publications, nor to Kandel. In the Teachers College *Educational Yearbook*, which Kandel edited, diagrams of education systems had been included sporadically and in an unsystematic form in a small number of contributions from the 1924 yearbook onwards (Stokvis, 1925, p. 236; Lee, 1929, p. 445; Příhoda, 1931, p. 167; Rivers-Smith, 1932, p. 169). In the earlier 1918 *Comparative Education: studies of the educational systems of six modern nations*, which Kandel edited with William Fletcher Russell, Peter Sandiford and Arthur H. Hope (Russell et al, 1918), Kandel's chapter on Germany included a prototype diagram of the Organisation of Prussian Higher Girls' Schools, similar in style to a diagram in Paul Monroe's (1911) *Cyclopedia of Education* (vol. 3, p. 86). Two other chapters in *Comparative Education* included diagrams: Russell for the United States (Russell et al, 1918, pp. 77-78) and Sandiford for England (pp. 252, 266). But diagrams were not included systematically, nor was each country represented in the systematic way in which Kandel (1933) used diagrams in his *Comparative Education* (see Figure 7) and which his research student Yoshi Kasuya would employ in her 1933 comparative study of the secondary education of girls in England, Germany, the United States and Japan (Kasuya, 1933). In Kandel's publication and that of Kasuya, diagrams were included for each education system and the forms of representation were systematic.

At Teachers College, Kandel had been aware of the attempts made at the IBE to develop a common international system of educational records and reports. He thought that longer term, it might be possible to secure some international standards in educational statistics and that it might be possible eventually to evolve methods for reducing statistics to common standards.

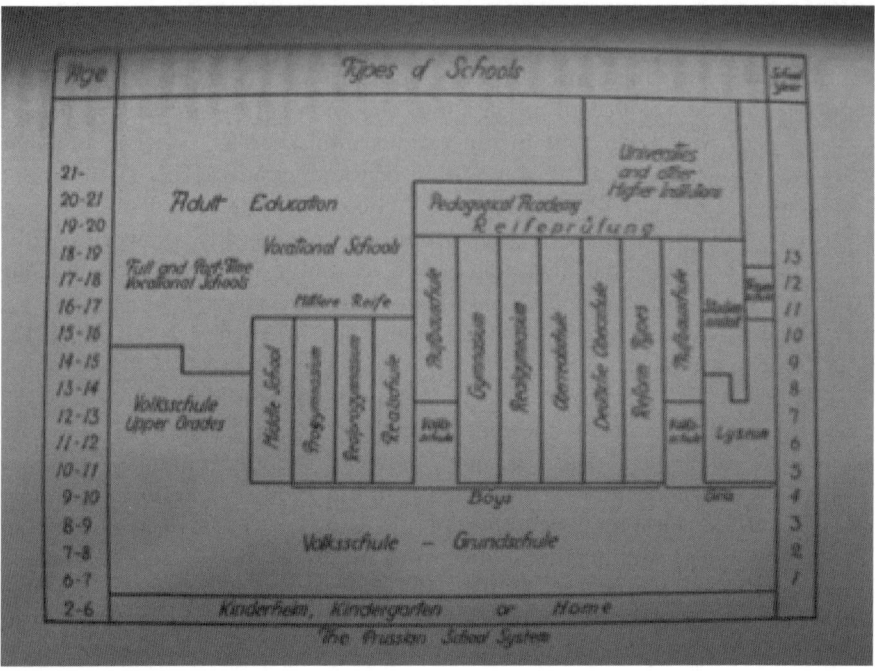

Figure 7. The Prussian school system (Kandel, 1933, p. 141).

But he was critical of treating education as an objective science to be progressed by statistical methods. He argued that, assuming that the methods of statistical tests and measurements had become sufficiently established to be reliable, all that it would be possible to claim for them was that they could measure results. But it would not be possible to use statistics to define the aims and purposes of education. Statistical methods might be used to formulate norms but only in a limited range of activities. But they could not set up qualitative standards, and they ignored the fact that education was a social process that was increasingly being organised on a national basis (Kandel, 1933, p. xxiii).

Kandel thought that the development of education as a science was possible, but only in a very limited sense because both the human element and human relations were too complex to be as easily defined and measured for educational purposes as some enthusiasts for a science of education would claim (p. 21). He maintained this was particularly the case for international statistics, where uniformity of standards had not yet been achieved (p. xxiv). While educational statisticians might measure results in different countries by the same system of tests, what could be measured

130

represented on the whole only the rudiments of an education and he was doubtful whether the quality of education could ever be measured (p. xiv). In addition, statistics were frequently not available for the same year and, in the absence of an international index of the cost of living, he viewed it as futile to attempt to compare figures for the cost of education, for salaries or per capita expenditures, for the length of school year varied in different countries, and there was an absence of uniformity in organisation (p. xxiv). At the heart of Kandel's critique of scientific approaches was his view that a study of foreign school systems which neglected the search for the hidden meaning of things found in the schools, and which failed to take into account ways in which national sentiment was embedded in education systems, would be of little value as a contribution to the clarification of thought, to the better development of education as science and to the formulation of a comprehensive, all-embracing philosophy of education thoroughly rooted in the culture, ideals and aspirations by which each nation should seek to add to the store of human welfare (p. xxv).

For her part, Arató, too, had considered national sentiment, particularly in her discussion of education for girls in England and Italy. She was aware of developments at Teachers College, having visited the Child Development Institute at Teachers College, and the Speyer and Horace Mann schools, as part of her research. Arató's diagrams, while used systematically and using a systematic form of representation, shared some characteristics with the representation of the Prussian Higher Girls' Schools in Paul Monroe's (1911) *Cyclopedia of Education* (vol. 3, p. 86), which was also similar in style to Kandel's diagram in his chapter on Germany in *Comparative Education: studies of the educational systems of six modern nations* (Russell et al, 1918, p. 161).

In the next section, I conclude by exploring how graphic representation of education systems in comparative education texts like Arató's contain linear concepts of time, past, present and future, and compress the cultural, biographical systems in which educational systems have their *longue durée*.[11] I argue that, removed from their location in national landscapes, diagrams of education systems become amenable to multiple readings as they cross national borders. I also consider tensions in comparative education texts.

Conclusion: locationless logic, comparative education and 'progress' in girls' secondary education

The majority of *L'Enseignement secondaire des jeunes filles en Europe* was forward looking as Arató followed her plan to illustrate the challenge for contemporary women of the best means to create education worthy of fulfilling the ambitions of the 'modern woman' (Arató, 1934, p. 29). Her text demonstrates Popkewitz's claim that the notion of 'progress' focuses on recent actions in the name of shedding past traditions in order to create something new and different (Popkewitz, 2005, pp. 22-25), and it exemplifies his view that the production of new moral values was seen to entail destabilising the past and 'emptying' history. It also illustrates what Popkewitz terms the 'hope' of science as a cultural thesis for modes of everyday living (Popkewitz, 2006, p. 150).

Mike Savage argues that new research techniques were not simply a matter of scientific 'progress', or the advancement of knowledge, but involved the remaking of politics and culture through new understandings of time and space through the deployment of myriad classifications, social aggregates and abstract territorial entities, which brought about new possibilities for imagining social entities and nations (Savage, 2010, p. vii). Savage highlights how such repertoires enable 'now time' to be 'seized away from the embrace of a differentially constituted past' (p. 237). He notes that this is not simply a matter of scientific progress or the advance of knowledge but is related to the remaking of future hierarchies crystallised through a mode of knowing in the image of a social scientific methodology (p. 237). In this sense, Arató's visualisations can be interpreted as repertoires that 'wrench' the recent away from a relationship with the past.

Arató's visualisations are also spatial systems in themselves and have a spatial aspect. Here, as Savage notes in relation to his discussion of inscription devices, the work of Marilyn Strathern on literalisation is instructive. By literalisation, Strathern (1990) refers to making things transparent 'through a mode of laying out the coordinates or conventional points of reference of what is otherwise taken for granted' (Savage, 2010, p. 13). Strathern argues that, as an engine of change, making the implicit explicit as a mode of constructing knowledge has relied on obscuring other features. Applying Strathern's framing to Arató's visualisations suggests that Arató's visualisations occlude and obscure ways in which they abstract from the historical, cultural and physical landscape in which forms of power and expertise are said to reside. For Arató's visualisations, this creates what Mitchell (2002) calls 'locationless logic', in which claims of expertise are constituted with no reference to any conception of place. Savage (2010, p. 14) notes that this lack of context means that a 'sameness' supplies a logic that becomes the source of historical movement and the motor of social transformation. In this process academic disciplines, and bodies of statistical and theoretical knowledge, have all played a part (pp. 246, 271).

In terms of 'reading' visualisations, Bruner (1966) points to the logic-like or 'rational' quality of adult human conceptualising. He argues that people use only minimal cues provided by split-second presentation of stimuli, but use them as a platform from which to leap to highly predictable conclusions. Much of perception, he argues, involves going beyond the information given through reliance on a model of the world of events that makes possible interpolation, extrapolation and prediction (p. 2). This is the case for what he calls the use of summarising images in which representation is governed by principles of perceptual organisation. Here, 'economical transformations' in perceptual organisation involve techniques for filling in and completing extrapolations based on forms of habituation. In this process, he argues, images develop an autonomous status, they become great summarisers of action (p. 17). This resonates with an 'actor–network' approach to materialist readings that relates to modes of inscription as well as to a materialist concern to render the (occluded) landscape in all its forms and inscriptions as an active social agent linked with aspects of social identity (Savage, 2010, p. 14).[12]

Insights from Bulmer, Mitchell, Strathern and Bruner suggest that visualisations are amenable to crossing national borders because they are emptied of history, abstracted from the landscape via the process of 'locationless logic' and interpolated in a new context through filling in and completing extrapolations based on forms of habituation. This provides a potential glimpse into the process by which visualisations of girls' education like Arató's might be read in some countries through an interpretation of girls' education as a conservative force, while in some countries they might be read through interpretations that have seen girls' education as a force for change, whether within democratic or authoritarian political agendas (Albisetti et al, 2010, p. 4). On the one hand, scientisation of knowledge underpinned by cooperative internationalism, and enhanced by visualisations, held the promise of 'progress'; on the other, it could also shore up 'tradition'.

Arató's *L'Enseignement secondaire des jeunes filles en Europe* illustrates how a concern with historical background and national characteristics can run counter to visual inscription devices that occlude the characteristics an author might seek to reveal. The complexities in Arató's text, with its data inscriptions and visualisations, provide a salutary lesson for policy-makers seeking to use international comparative data for contemporary education policy purposes; for there is no easy reading on which to base prescription.

Notes

[1] Historical accounts that include an international perspective on education for women and girls include Stanton (1884), International Council of Women (1911) and Kasuya (1933).

[2] Diagrams of education systems also play into Martin Lawn's question in the seminar, 'What is an education system?'.

[3] Arató was a secondary teacher from Budapest who received her doctorate from the Sorbonne. For the two years of her research, Arató's salary was paid by the Hungarian Ministry of Education. Charles Little, who came across Arató in conversation with Dr Isabella Grassi (president of the Italian Federation of University Women) while researching in Italy in 1932, described Arató, as 'Amelie Arató, Docteur Lettres (seemingly from a French University), who lives in Budapest' (Little, 1932, p. 81).

[4] Nemeth discusses the rise of educational sciences in Hungary and notes that by the interwar period, Conservative political tendencies had pushed qualifications for teachers in Hungary upwards to the point of requiring qualified teachers to have successfully completed courses and seminars at the university and at the teacher education institution (Nemeth, 2006, p. 170).

[5] Replies to the earlier survey were received from Australia, Austria, Belgium, Bulgaria, Canada, Czecho-Slovakia, Denmark, Finland, France, Great Britain, Holland, India, Ireland, Italy, New Zealand, Norway, Sweden, Switzerland and the United States (IFUW, 1925, p. 43).

[6] Wendland (2011) notes that in the Baltic states, the German perspective was replaced by national narratives in the interwar period, when a cultural definition of nation was the most adequate in the case of non-dominant nations without historical statehood (Latvians) whereas Lithuania scholars would refer to the historical state traditions of a more distant past (the Grand Duchy of Lithuania).

[7] While Arató paid attention to national minorities, 'nation' itself was not interrogated in her text in terms of the position of women within the 'national awakening' within the Baltic states prior to the First World War, which fed into claims for national self-determination on the part of minorities. In Latvia, for example, Novikova (2000, pp. 329-330) argues that the leaders of the national awakening proposed nationalism as the emancipating ideology of equality and human rights that would in time change the status of the nation as well as of women in the struggle against oppression.

[8] Popkewitz (2006, p. 162) notes that to speak of overlapping practices is not to argue unities of process or causation.

[9] See also Goodman (2010, 2012). Cooperative internationalism overlooked questions of power and national self-interest (Fritz, 2005, pp. 142-144).

[10] There was some diversity in quality and quantity of information between countries, for information from ministries was edited as little as possible; and for some countries there were multiple entries, as in the case of Australia, where different areas of states operated different education systems, which resulted in the inclusion of 61 diagrams for 53 countries (IBE, 1933, p. vi).

[11] Analysis here draws on Cowan (2000, p. 341; 2002, pp. 417, 420).

[12] Here, Savage (2010) builds on Green (2005) and Steedman (1986).

References

Albisetti, J.C., Goodman, J. & Rogers, R. (2010) Girls' Secondary Education in the Western World: a historical introduction, in J.C. Albisetti, J. Goodman & R. Rogers (Eds) *Girls' Secondary Education in the Western World: from the 18th to the 20th century.* New York: Palgrave.

Arató, A. (1934) *L'Enseignement secondaire des jeunes filles en Europe* [The secondary education of girls in Europe]. Brussels: Anc. Établiss. J. Lebegue & Cie.

Boyd Rayward, W. (2008) European Modernism and the Information Society: introduction, in W. Boyd Rayward (Ed.) *European Modernism and the Information Society: informing the present, understanding the past*, pp. 1-26. Aldershot: Ashgate.

Bruner, J.S. (1966) *Toward a Theory of Instruction.* Cambridge, MA: Belknap Press of Harvard University Press.

Cowan, R. (2000) Comparing Futures or Comparing Pasts? *Comparative Education*, 36(3), 333-342.

Cowan, R. (2002) Moments of Time: a comparative note, *History of Education*, 31(5), 413-424.

Eley, G. (2000) Culture, Nation and Gender, in I. Blom, K. Hagemann & C. Hall (Eds) *Gendered Nations: nationalisms and gender order in the long nineteenth century*, pp. 27-40. Oxford: Berg.

Fritz, J.S. (2005) Internationalism and the Promise of Science, in D. Long & B.C. Schmidt (Eds) *Imperialism and Internationalism in the Discipline of International Relations*, pp. 141-158. New York: SUNY.

Goodman, J. (2002) A Historiography of Founding Fathers? Sarah Austin (1793-1867) and English Comparative Education, *History of Education*, 31(5), 425-435.

Goodman, J. (2010) Cosmopolitan Women Educators, 1920-1939, Inside/Outside Activism and Abjection, *Paedagogica Historica*, 46(1-2), 69-83.

Goodman, J. (2011) International Citizenship and the International Federation of University Women before 1939, *History of Education*, 40(6), 701-721.

Goodman, J. (2012) Women and International Intellectual Co-operation, *Paedagogica Historica*, 48(3), 357-368.

Green, S. (2005) *Notes from the Balkans: locating marginality and ambiguity on the Greek-Albanian border.* Princeton, NJ: Princeton University Press.

Hartmann, F. (2008) Visualizing Social Facts: Otto Neurath's ISOTYPE Project, in W. Boyd Rayward (Ed.) *European Modernism and the Information Society: informing the present, understanding the past*, pp. 279-294. Aldershot: Ashgate.

Hupchick, D.P. & Cox, H.E. (2001) *The Palgrave Concise Historical Atlas of Eastern Europe.* New York: Palgrave.

IBE (International Bureau of Education) (1929a) The Activity of the Bureau, Report No. 15, *Bulletin of the IBE*, no. 12, June 1929. Geneva: IBE.

IBE (International Bureau of Education) (1929b) The Activity of the Bureau, Report No. 16, *Bulletin of the IBE*, no. 13, September 1929. Geneva: IBE.

IBE (International Bureau of Education) (1930a) Organisation of the International Bureau of Education, *Bulletin of the IBE*, no. 14, January 1930, Year IV, no. 1, 1930. Geneva: IBE.

IBE (International Bureau of Education) (1930b) School Organisation Section, in Activity of the Bureau During the Third Quarter of the Year 1930, *Bulletin of the International Bureau of Education*, no. 15, April 1930, Year IV, no. 2, 6-7.

IBE (International Bureau of Education) (1931a) School Organisation Section, in Activity of the Bureau During the Last Quarter of the Year 1930, *Bulletin of the International Bureau of Education*, no. 18, January 1931, Year V, no. 1, 4.

IBE (International Bureau of Education) (1931b) Information Division, in Activity of the Bureau During the Last Quarter of the Year 1930, *Bulletin of the International Bureau of Education*, no. 18, January 1931, Year V, no. 1, 5-6.

IBE (International Bureau of Education) (1931c) School Organisation Section, in Activity of the Bureau During the First Quarter of the Year 1931, *Bulletin of the International Bureau of Education*, no. 19, April 1931, Year IV, no. 2, 44.

IBE (International Bureau of Education) (1931d) School Organisation Section, in Activity of the Bureau During the Second Quarter of the Year 1930, *Bulletin of the International Bureau of Education*, no. 20, July 1931, Year V, no. 3, 90.

IBE (International Bureau of Education) (1931e) Information Division, in Activity of the Bureau During the Second Quarter of the Year 1930, *Bulletin of the International Bureau of Education*, no. 20, July 1931, Year V, no. 3, 90-91.

IBE (International Bureau of Education) (1933) *L'Organisation de l'instruction publique dans 53 pays* [The organisation of public instruction in 53 countries]. Geneva: IBE.

IBE (International Bureau of Education) (n.d.) *Plan for the Classification of Educational Documents*. Geneva: IBE.

IFUW (International Federation of University Women) (1925) *Report of the Council Meeting in Brussels, July 1925*. London: IFUW.

IFUW (International Federation of University Women) (1930) *Fifteenth Council Meeting – Prague, July 1930*. London: IFUW.

International Council of Women (1911) *National Systems of Education. First Report of the Education Committee of the International Council of Women, Compiled by Mrs Ogilvie Gordon*. Aberdeen: Rosemount Press.

Kandel, I. (1918) Germany, in W.F. Russell, P. Sandiford, I. Kandel & A.H. Hope (Eds) *Comparative Education: studies of the educational systems of six modern nations*, pp. 107-182. London: J.M. Dent & Sons.

Kandel, I. (1933) *Comparative Education*. London: George G. Harrap & Co.

Kasuya, Y. (1933) *A Comparative Study of the Secondary Education of Girls in England, Germany and the United States, with a Consideration of the Secondary Education of Girls in Japan*. New York: Teachers College, Columbia University.

Lee, E.A. (1929) United States, in I. Kandel (Ed.) *Educational Yearbook of the International Institute of Teachers College Columbia University, 1928*, pp. 393-453. New York: Macmillan.

Little, C.E. (1932) The Italians and their Schools, *Peabody Journal of Education*, 19(2), 72-86.

Livingstone, D. (2005) *Putting Science in its Place: geographies of scientific knowledge*. Chicago: University of Chicago Press.

Mitchell, T. (2002) *The Rule of Experts: Egypt, techno-politics, modernity*. Berkeley: University of California Press.

Monroe, P. (1911) *Cyclopedia of Education*, vol. 3. New York: Macmillan (1914 edition).

Nemeth, A. (2006) A Chapter in the History of an Ambivalent Relationship: connections between the new education movement outside of the universities and academic pedagogy in Hungary, in R. Hofstetter & B. Schneuwly (Eds) *Passion*,

Fusion, Tension: new education and educational sciences end 19th- middle 20th century, pp. 169-189. Bern: Peter Lang.

Nikolow, S. (2008) *Gesellschaft und Wirtschaft*: an encyclopedia in Otto Neurath's pictorial statistics from 1930, in W. Boyd Rayward (Ed.) *European Modernism and the Information Society: informing the present, understanding the past* (pp. 257-278). Aldershot: Ashgate.

Novikova, I. (2000) Constructing National Identity in Latvia: gender and representation during the period of the national awakening, in I. Blom, K. Hagemann & C. Hall (Eds) *Gendered Nations: nationalisms and gender order in the long nineteenth century*, pp. 311-334. Oxford: Berg.

Otlet, P. & Oderfeld, A. (1929) *Atlas de la civilisation universelle. Conception – Organisation – Méthodes de la préparation du matériel didactique en coopération international par Paul Otlet et Anne Oderfeld* [Atlas of universal civilisation. Conception – Organisation – Methods of preparing teaching material in international cooperation by Paul Otlet and Anne Oderfeld]. Brussels: Palais Mondial.

Phillips, D. & Schweisfurth, M. (2007) *Comparative and International Education: an introduction to theory, method and practice*. London: Continuum.

Popkewitz, T. (2005) Inventing the Modern Self and John Dewey: modernities and the traveling of pragmatism in education – An introduction, in T. Popkewitz (Ed.) *Inventing the Modern Self and John Dewey*, pp. 3-38. Basingstoke: Palgrave.

Popkewitz, T. (2006) The Idea of Science as Planning was not Planned. A Historical Note about American Pedagogical Sciences as (Re)Making Society and Individuality, in R. Hofstetter & B. Schneuwly (Eds) *Passion, Fusion, Tension: new education and educational sciences end 19th-middle 20th century*, pp. 143-167. Bern: Peter Lang.

Příhoda, V. (1931) Czechoslovakia, in I. Kandel (Ed.) *Educational Yearbook of the International Institute of Teachers College Columbia University, 1930*, pp. 161-184. New York: Macmillan.

Rivers-Smith, R. (1932) Education in the Tanganiyka Territory, in I. Kandel (Ed.) *Educational Yearbook of the International Institute of Teachers College Columbia University, 1931*, pp. 141-200. New York: Macmillan.

Rogers, R. (2006) Learning to be Good Girls and Women: education, training and schools, in D. Simonton (Ed.) *The Routledge History of Women in Europe since 1700*. London: Routledge.

Rossello, P. (1944) *Forerunners of the International Bureau of Education*. Abridged and translated by Marie Butts. London: Evans in association with the University of London Institute of Education.

Russell, W.F., Sandiford, P., Kandel, I. & Hope, A.H. (Eds) (1918) *Comparative Education: studies of the educational systems of six modern nations*. London: J.M. Dent & Sons.

Savage, M. (2010) *Identities and Social Change in Britain since 1940: the politics of method*. Oxford: Oxford University Press.

Sluga, G. (2006) *The Nation, Psychology and International Politics, 1870-1919*. Basingstoke: Palgrave.

Stanton, T. (Ed.) (1884) *The Woman Question in Europe. A Series of Original Essays.* New York: Putnam.

Steedman, C. (1986) *Landscape for a Good Woman.* London: Virago.

Stokvis, Z. (1925) Dutch East Indies, in I. Kandel (Ed.) *Educational Yearbook of the International Institute of Teachers College Columbia University 1924*, pp. 233-258. New York: Macmillan.

Strathern, M. (1990) *After Nature. English Kinship in the Late Twentieth Century.* Oxford: Clarendon Press.

Van den Heuvel, C. (2008) Building Society, Constructing Knowledge, Weaving the Web: Otlet's visualizations of a global information society and his concept of a universal civilisation, in W. Boyd Rayward (Ed.) *European Modernism and the Information Society: informing the present, understanding the past*, pp.127–154. Aldershot: Ashgate.

Wendland, A.V. (2011) The Russian Empire and its Western Borderlands: national historiographies and their 'others' in Russia, the Baltics and the Ukraine, in S. Berger & C. Lorenz (Eds) *The Contested Nation: ethnicity, class, religion and gender in national histories*, pp. 405-441. Basingstoke: Palgrave.

Governing Population: the emergence of a political arithmetic of inequalities in education. A Comparison between the United Kingdom and France

ROMUALD NORMAND

SUMMARY Based on a comparative perspective between the United Kingdom (UK) and France, the chapter explores an important historical period in the quantification of inequalities in education. It starts with a presentation of the genesis and the development of the UK political arithmetic of inequalities embedded in a eugenic orthodoxy and issues of population policy and politics. It shows how some tools and concepts have travelled from psychology to sociology and then from the UK to France. The explanation for the increase in data cannot be separated from considerations about the extension of the Welfare State, searching for a compromise between economical effectiveness and social justice. The reader is invited to discover some links between science and politics, and the role of policy borrowing and knowledge transfer in the building of quantitative sociology of education as a discipline and science of government.

The measurement of inequalities in education supporting the intervention of the State, along theoretical and methodological assumptions, is the main focus of this chapter. Some psychological, economic and sociological studies have deepened the knowledge of school populations in order to build a compromise between economic effectiveness and social justice. Two comparative periods of time in the development of this quantification are presented in the following sections.

The first period concerns a novel scientific and political setting in the United Kingdom (UK) during the 1920s-30s. Eugenics promoted methods to improve the quality of the population alongside a demographic plan aiming to make talents more useful for economic development. The London

139

School of Economics and Political Science (LSE) was at the centre of this paradigm which led to the development of the quantitative sociology of education after the Second World War, as well as reforms in education and the institutionalisation of the Welfare State.

Controlling the population was also prominent in France during the same period. During the 1920s-30s, some circulation and translation of knowledge occurred between the UK and France, taking place in international conferences, visits and exchanges between scientists and policy-makers. Of course, the French fabrication of ideas and metrological tools took place within its own tradition established by Quetelet's statistics, Bertillon's anthropometrics and Binet-Simon's test (Desrosières, 1993; Normand, 2011). Stanley Hall's surveys had inspired the Société libre pour l'étude psychologique de l'enfant (Free Society for the Psychological Study of the Child), within which Ferdinand Buisson, Emile Durkheim and Alfred Binet were involved – albeit through different ways – in the study of the discipline, morals and psychological features of the child (Pinell, 1977).

There are no simple causal links in the circulation from the UK to France of ideas and the building of statistics supporting population politics and policy. Through knowledge transfer and policy borrowing, some international standards have been disseminated and adjusted to the French context. This chapter describes a particular French setting which offers some similarities with the political arithmetic of inequalities developed in the UK. I also demonstrate the importance of Anglo-American constituents in the building of the French measurements of the quantity and quality of the population. I then study their impact in the emergence of early quantitative works of the sociology of education.

Governing Population: the political arithmetic of the Welfare State in the UK

In studying the link between demography and degeneracy during the 1920s, the science of eugenics gained in legitimacy through the use of a specific discourse and the implementation of tools for measuring the quality of the population (Soloway, 1990). Eugenics had consequences for social policies, particularly in education, and the development of institutional and legal frameworks. The naturalness of the population, as Foucault argued, required an art of governing and a science of calculation, conjoining issues of medicine, public hygiene, demography and political economy (Foucault, 2004). A new State governmentality had to take into account natural phenomena (birth, fecundity, mortality) and to intervene and control populations but also serve the development of capitalism. The social questions concerning protection against disease, regeneration of the workforce, improvement of the human stock and fighting against waste called for a general improvement in economic efficiency according to new modes of redistribution and social justice. Gradually, the problematics of the Welfare

State emerged among intellectual and scientific circles close to the LSE. The thesis of a new political arithmetic of inequalities in education was gradually conceptualised while the demographic issue impacted on social policy and politics.

Eugenicist Theory and Social Surveys at the Beginning of British Sociology

Eugenics, following the works of Francis Galton, used knowledge about heredity and natural selection to create a biological science embedded in statistical measurements of intelligence. This conception of the stability and immutability of individual characters deeply influenced the research of British psychologists during the 1920s (Sutherland, 1984; Wooldridge, 1994). These assumptions were resumed by Karl Pearson. He led for many years the Galton Eugenics Laboratory (1907-13), which became the best-known centre of biometric research in the UK. This centre revolutionised the application of statistics through the compilation of voluminous data on populations. It was relayed by different journals: *Biometrika* (1901), devoted to the application of mathematics to biology, and created by Galton, Pearson and Weldon; the *Eugenic Review* (1912), in which Cyril Burt published his first paper on the inheritance of mental capacities; the *Annals of Eugenics* (1925), headed by Sir Ronald Fisher.

If eugenicist psychology was viewed as legitimised and recognised science, British sociology was, at its beginning, a 'discipline for rich amateurs' (Dahrendorf, 1995, pp. 94-107). Sociology tried to find a place between the biological and historical sciences by conducting empirical studies and being inspired by the first social surveys of Charles Booth and Benjamin S. Rowntree. The alliance between sociologists, social reformers and charities seemed evident. In 1904-05, the Sociological Society published its first conferences in an annual series named 'Sociological Papers'. The first papers began with a section on eugenics written by Francis Galton. He explained that eugenics had to be framed as a fundamental and applied research project to raise the average quality of the population and the civic value of citizens. If a few sociologists were reluctant to endorse these ideas, most of them agreed with Galton's assumptions. Some of contributors in the volume explained that women had to be aware of their natural impulsion to serve and sacrifice themselves. Others defended polygamy as a solution for eugenicist issues (in order to be independent of marriage and to ensure the best reproduction) or they sustained the sterilisation of losers in social competition to improve the human stock.

However, eugenics as the 'biological foundations of sociology' was not the only interest of the Sociological Society. Members were concerned with the development of applied sociology according to systematic surveys of 'civic facts'. William Beveridge, the founder of the British Welfare State, regularly attended these meetings. After the conversion of these 'Sociological Papers' into the *Sociological Review*, the discipline entered the LSE. During the first

141

half of the twentieth century, sociology was less influential than other academic disciplines (Dahrendorf, 1995, pp. 196-266). The social survey remained an affair of 'enlightened amateurs' outside the academic field (Bulmer, 1985). Some local and scattered studies were implemented. Only after the Second World War were a Government Social Survey and a Government Statistical Survey created (Whitehead, 1985). Meanwhile, social surveys were developed alongside the population census administered by the General Register Office since 1837. The collection of data was managed afterward Booth and Rowntree by businessmen who used their wealth to conduct surveys on urban poverty, housing and unemployment (Desrosières, 1993, pp. 272-276).

This work was continued from 1927 to 1932 at the LSE in the New Survey of London Life and Labour (Kent, 1985). At this time, it was the longer local survey that gave an account of social consequences of unemployment and the Great Depression. Another research strategy used randomised sampling applied to studies on poverty, but these ideas, expressed by Arthur L. Bowley in his book *Measurement of Social Phenomena* (1915), were not well received. At the beginning of the century, several researchers had also attempted to institutionalise the sociological discipline in the Sociological Society. They tried to bring together the civic sociology of Patrick Geddes, eugenicists, social worker trainees, and sociologists interested in philosophy and comparative studies. But tensions emerged between Geddes and Leonard T. Hobhouse, the editor of the *Sociological Review*, because of their competition over the chair of sociology at the LSE. Patrick Geddes disseminated the social theory of Frédéric Le Play but he translated it within an evolutionist framework and became a strong advocate for studying community and family alongside a naïve, messianic and ecological vision. 'Mass observation' was another kind of amateurism aiming to study human populations as birds (Calder, 1985). These isolated approaches, which were heavily criticised, could not resist the influence of statistical works developed by Galton, Pearson and Fisher. These eugenicists were decisive in the orientation of empirical studies focused on demographical issues. Under the leadership of William Beveridge, the LSE was also a place where statistical methods were emphasised in the scientific study of the population.

Quality versus Quantity of the Population: a social policy debate

The defeat of the British army during the Boer War (1899-1902) raised some concerns about the capacity of the 'British race' to face adversity. These doubts reached the school system, where local authorities reinforced medical inspections to prevent the deterioration of the race. Eugenicists, like Karl Pearson, thought these measures were insufficient because the problem was the diminution of capable and gifted people, e.g. the quality of the population. Malthusian theorists expressed other assumptions and considered it was a quantitative problem due to the excessive fertility of the poor. The former argued for social selection of the best and most capable individuals to stop the decline. The latter argued the remedy was contraception, self-responsibility and a decrease in family size. Eugenicists advocated the reinforcement of tools to measure innate capacities. Malthusians defended a rational and progressive intervention of the State in health and education.

New ideas, advanced by socialists and liberals, argued that the deterioration of the situation of the poor could be counterbalanced by social programmes (Soloway, 1990, pp. 163-192). Pearson and most eugenicists promoted the strict application of biological and natural laws, but Malthusians supported an extension of social legislation to protect childhood. Even as fervent a eugenicist as Ronald A. Fisher proposed that the reconstruction of the race could be accelerated by adjusted pensions, bonuses for marriage, family allowances and tax cuts for talented individuals. William Beveridge sustained the principle of family allowances and salary supplements to encourage birth. While Karl Pearson's assumptions were more and more disputed, some studies demonstrated a positive correlation between increase in salaries and improvement in the health, vitality and productivity of the labour force.

Taking into account this public climate, eugenicists, despite some resistance, joined the Malthusians' thesis, and sought to promote 'positive eugenics' by studying the relationship between eugenics and demography (Soloway, 1990, pp. 193-202). In his book *The Population Problems* (1922), Carr-Saunders questioned the hereditary differences between social classes and argued that success, as a measurement of eugenic value, was mostly dependent on sociological conditions and not on the innate capacities of individuals. Carlos P. Blacker, the General Secretary of the Eugenics Society, in his book *Birth Control and the State* (1926), proposed a survey on contraception to the Minister of Health. A year later, the Society created a Birth Control Investigation Committee, including researchers and physicians, to examine the effects of contraception on the physical, mental and racial health of the population. The Society's commitment to the control of birth rates was a landmark in the shift from propaganda to politics and policy planning related to demographic issues. It also brought new ideas to the relationship between heredity and environment.

The London School of Economics and the
Emergence of a Political Arithmetic in Education

At the LSE, the first studies related to the question of poverty. Then, under the leadership of William Beveridge, they were extended to the analysis of society and social problems (Scot, 2005). The natural sciences remained the model of social sciences and a great interest was expressed in economics, statistics and social biology. Research was mainly empirical and based on measurement and quantification. Of course, there were also literary disciplines such as philosophy, sociology and history. Richard Tawney, the founder of the history of economics at the LSE, gave numerous lectures on the issue of equality. He wrote two books, *Secondary Education for All* (1922) and *Equality* (1931), which strongly impacted on the Labour Party's education strategy. Tawney criticised the hereditary vision of education and its organisation through social classes, which, for him, created injustice and waste. He wanted to facilitate the access of working-class children to secondary education and to abandon early selection.

However, statistics and demographic sciences occupied a main position in the scientific architecture of the LSE. Eugenicists, using IQ tests, medical examinations and anthropometrical measurements, wondered if the extent of deterioration or degeneracy could be calculated to regulate the 'human stock'. However, from regional surveys he had led on fertility, Beveridge considered that the relatively unfit were in better health now than before the War. For him, there was no evidence of a deterioration in their physical and mental conditions (Soloway, 1990). This argument was taken over by two other economists, A.L. Bowey and M.H. Hogg, who demonstrated a strong correlation between the increase in salaries and health. The increase in salaries seemed more effective than the reduction in family size to fight against poverty. Consequently, criticism was addressed against eugenic assumptions by a group of sociologists and biologists working at the LSE in the Department of Social Biology, created in 1925 by the Rockefeller Foundation.

The US foundation had allocated funds to create the department and to develop research in biology and social sciences at the LSE. William Beveridge appointed Lancelot Hogben as its first director (Wooldridge, 1994, pp. 263-270). The department aimed to promote a new 'political arithmetic' in investigating the measurement of population quality and fighting against the waste of resources. Beveridge was persuaded that 'bio-economics' could renew the methodologies of the social sciences. For him, the application of biology to human society would cover varied areas such as human instincts, innate and acquired character, quantity and quality of the population, economic and racial health tests, etc. Hogben was one of the most brilliant biologists of his time. His concern for a 'neutral science on an ethical ground' opposed him to the tradition of eugenics. He wanted to break with a purely biological approach within demography and to move towards social issues. In 1938, his memorandum *Political Arithmetic* proposed coordinating a research project devoted to the issue of population, and compiling research on fertility, mortality, family structure, human capacities and equality of opportunities.

Hogben criticised the assumptions of psychometrics and the measurement of IQ, whereas he considered the environment had to be taken seriously to explain social stratification. But he was also arguing for a planned elimination of undesirable types and characters in society. However, he defended a research project presented by J.L. Gray and Pearl Moshinsky, two researchers at the Department of Social Biology, in their radical criticism of the psychometric orthodoxy (Hogben, 1938). They studied the link between IQ and equality of access to education and demonstrated that Cyril Burt's work was biased. This criticism was taken up by J.L. Gary in his book *The Nation's Intelligence* (1936), which estimated that the link between IQ and social position was not firmly established because of varied social circumstances bearing on the genesis of intellectual qualities. At the same time, other researchers distanced themselves from eugenics and Malthusian assumptions because they thought the threat to national well-being could be explained by the decline in fertility (Blacker & Glass, 1937). Their research interests shifted from eugenics to issues of population planning and regulation of birth rates.

David Glass, the successor to Lancelot Hogben, was appointed Professor of Demography at the LSE. He was a sort of mediation between eugenics and the sociology of social mobility. He was persuaded that social mobility had to contribute to a new meritocratic order and to increase economic effectiveness through a better use of human capacities (Glass, 1954). In this intellectual climate, Floud et al (1956) began a study on the role of social selection in education. From a measurement of IQ, through a comparison of their research findings with those of Gray and Moshinsky, they showed that working-class pupils were the losers in schooling despite an equivalent IQ. Like Glass, they considered that the choice of another mechanism of selection would serve social justice and economic effectiveness. They defended the comprehensive school because they thought it would enhance social mobility, reduce waste and lead towards a more egalitarian society (Halsey et al, 1961). Following the tradition of political arithmetic, Halsey continued to study social mobility by measuring the effects of IQ and social class on school achievement.

Sciences and Politics of the French Population: some epistemic translations of Anglo-American tools and concepts

The control of population was also at stake in the French public debate in the earlier twentieth century. Some intellectuals were resisting the decadence of French society and the decline analysed through demographic statistics, particularly the decrease in birth rates (Schneider, 1990, pp. 11-54). Between the two world wars, a State eugenic policy, through a compromise between hygienic ideas and pro-natalist ones, developed statistics supported by institutions and associations involved in public education and health. The modern government of the French population was supported by the importation of methods and tools invented in the UK and the USA in new disciplines like psychometrics, biometrics and political arithmetic. This orientation was confirmed during the Vichy regime, and reinforced after the Second World War once contacts with British and US circles had been resumed. Marshall Funds and the implementation of social planning created an opportunity to renew the metrological apparatus of the State. In this section I will describe the emergence of this State planning based on the methodology of large-scale surveys designed before the War, and the epistemic and methodological transfer from the USA and the UK to France. We will observe that the technology of French large-scale surveys was implemented in the field of education and close to the political arithmetic of inequalities conceptualised in the UK.

Pro and Cons of Eugenics in the Quest
for Quantity and Quality of the Population

At the beginning of the twentieth century, Malthusians and pro-natalist defenders were sharing contrasting views on the means to regenerate the population. Malthusians, who were associated closely with the socialists and the Republican Leagues, and were advocates of social hygiene, wanted couples who were educated to fight against disease and poor health to decide for themselves about their procreation. Pro-natalist activists, in the camp of Catholic partisans, defended State intervention to encourage families to give birth to more children through an advantageous tax system, subsidies, marriage loans and the creation of an electoral system which would take into account the size of the household. On the side of pro-natalist activists, the statistician Jacques Bertillon, the physiologist Charles Richet and the Member of Parliament André Honnorat created in 1896 the Alliance nationale pour l'accroissement de la population française (National Alliance for the Growth of the French Population). In 1902, they obtained the creation of a parliamentary commission on depopulation. This commission had to conduct a general study and to propose solutions. In their report *The Moral and Sociological Causes of Depopulation* (Bulletin de l'alliance nationale pour l'accroissement de la population française, 1902), Bertillon and Honnorat argued that parents' egotism and ambition for their children were the major causes of the decline in birth rates. Lucien March, who was a very well-known demographer and the General Director of the Statistique générale de France, had worked with the commission. He was sustaining the assumptions of Adolphe Pinard, the inventor of infant care in France, who was investigating issues of social heredity and quality of the population. However, the ideas of Galton were not hitherto well known in France except by a few physicians.

Things changed after the participation of March, Pinard and other scientists at the International Conference of Eugenics in London (1912). After the conference, the French Society of Eugenics was created. Léon Bourgeois, the founder of solidarism and former president of the Ligue de l'enseignement (League of Education) and Minister of Labour, accepted the honorary presidency of the society. Meanwhile, March had become a fervent admirer of Galton and he presented demographic and statistical studies at

146

several international conferences. He was very familiar with the research of the eugenicists Pearson and Davenport. He translated Pearson's book *Grammar of Science*. From its creation, the French Society of Eugenics brought together eminent experts on demographic issues. The consultative committee, created after the London conference, had expressed a keen interest in eugenics and the French delegation had been the most important group among all of the other countries. The consultative committee included influential individuals: members of parliament but also biologists and physicians because of the weight of the medical profession in issues related to the degeneracy and reproduction of populations. The French Society of Eugenics, born in the amphitheatre of the École de Médecine in Paris, wanted to be a place like Pearson's laboratory at the University of London or the Eugenics Record Office, headed by Charles Davenport at Long Island. But, because of the First World War, this research unit was not created even though the Society extended its audience across numerous conferences.

In France, the assumptions underlying debate were different from those of British eugenics and Pearson. Members of the French Society of Eugenics were advocating 'positive eugenics' and were concerned with social hygiene. Public opinion thought that the First World War had created adverse selection and that the unfit had remained outside the battlefield while the most robust had perished. So France had to reconstruct and improve its population for the following generations. Lucien March was opposed to the vision developed in the UK that assumed a decline in the quality of the population and lower innate capacities within poor families. Like his colleagues, he favoured a policy which could increase the quantity of the population. But in the 1930s, French eugenics shifted to more negative recommendations such as prenuptial examination, restriction of immigration and control of births. Eugenicists no longer considered the necessity to improve the quantity of the population because they were challenged by the movement for mental hygiene and the fight against venereal disease. The Ligue des droits de l'homme (League of Human Rights) justified control of births in case motherhood was dangerous for mothers and for the future of the race. One of the spokesmen for these theories was Just Sicard de Plauzoles, the President of the French National League against the Venereal Peril. He explained that the role of eugenics was to maintain the best production of 'human capital' and that social hygiene had to obtain the best return on human investment. This vision was largely shared by French hygienists. Sicard de Plauzoles warned about the potential decline in the quality of the French population and its degeneracy because of diseases (alcoholism, syphilis, tuberculosis, etc.) and some evident signs of physical, moral and intellectual inferiority among working-class children. His Association d'études sexologiques (Association for Sexological Studies), associated closely with the Republican Leagues, replaced progressively the French Society of Eugenics in the public debate related to demographic issues while French eugenicists moved closer to their US counterparts.

147

During the Vichy regime, another French eugenicist, Alexis Carrel, created the Fondation pour l'étude des problèmes humains (Foundation for the Study of Human Problems). After 30 years spent in the USA, at the Rockefeller Institute for Medical Research, Carrel published his book, *Man, the Unknown* (1935), within which he defended eugenicist assumptions. The aim of the Foundation was to study appropriate measures to safeguard, improve and develop the French population. Research teams had to investigate different phases of human development (hereditary biology, birth rates, child development, living conditions). Carrel's theory was continued after the Second World War by a new generation of demographers and geneticists (Rosental, 2003). In March 1945, in the Foundation's journal, Robert Gessain and Paul Vincent wrote a paper titled 'Some Quantitative and Qualitative Aspects of the French Population', in which they argued that the potential of the population could be improved according to eugenic principles. Alfred Sauvy, the father of French demographics, and Director of the National Institute of Demographic Studies (which absorbed the Carrel Foundation in 1945), shared these ideas. Before the War, he had written about his concerns related to the quality of the population through arguments mixing social Darwinism and Lamarckism (Halbwachs & Sauvy, 1936). He argued that the increase in the quantity of the population could stimulate its quality. The new statutes of the National Institute of Demographic Studies envisaged that experiments would be conducted and information gathered to contribute to the quantitative growth and qualitative improvement of the population. In 1950, one of Alfred Sauvy's colleagues had devoted an entire volume to the issue of eugenics in the new journal *Population* (Sutter, 1950).

School Population Surveys and the Creation
of State Institutions of Planning and Statistics

Before the Second World War, the US Memorial Laura Spelman Fund, which had supported the creation of the LSE, wanted to develop a new generation of researchers in the French area of social sciences (Mazon, 1988). According to the Rockefeller Foundation's representatives who had studied the French context, French intellectual production was considered to be good quality but relatively scattered and French social sciences lacked resources and coordination. The Foundation proposed the creation of an institute of social sciences similar to the LSE. Charles Merriam, the US political scientist at the University of Chicago mandated by the Foundation, contacted Marcel Mauss, the sociologist, and Charles Rist, the economist, and asked them to submit a project. Although Charles Rist rose to the challenge and created an Institut de recherches économiques et sociales (Institute for Economic and Social Research), Mauss's project was dismissed by the Foundation because it was too large, even though he proposed something close to what would later become the Maison des sciences de l'homme (House of Social Sciences) in Paris. But Mauss was suspect because of his leftist and socialist aspirations and allegiances. However, some funds were allocated by Rockfeller to the Institute of Ethnology, in which Lucien Lévy-Bruhl and Marcel Mauss were working, and to the Centre of Social Documentation, headed by Célestin Bouglé. Some exchanges were also developed with the USA, particularly with the Institute of Chicago for Social Sciences. The US Foundation's requirements influenced the work of Bouglé, who wanted to move French sociology towards more empirical and experimental work to solve economic, political and sociological problems. Rockefeller funds were welcome among the community of French sociologists. For the first time money was available to develop surveys, field work and collective research projects. If an institution in social sciences had been created before the Second World War, it would have been influenced by these US methodological and positivist requirements. However, after the War, most of the representatives of Durkheim's sociology had disappeared.

In the field of psychology, researchers worked on guidance and professional selection from the measurement of innate capacities in different professions. Some psychologists such as Édouard Toulouse were in favour of the creation of a bureau of education and they defended the need to adopt rational means to examine systematically the school population. For them, bio-typology as a new discipline had to extend the area of psychometrics to invent a 'human classification' of characters. Toulouse, like his colleague Henri Laugier, was inspired by British biometrics and he wanted to use modern statistics to inventory variables and to classify and sort individuals. This scientific psychology, developed within the French Society of Bio-typology, attracted famous psychologists (Piéron, Lahy, Laugier, Weinberg, Wallon) and also anthropologists and statisticians. It was supported by intellectuals closely associated with socialist thought and freemasonry. They considered that professional guidance was a means to implement a rational order to increase the value of individuals and allocate them to fair social positions. The efficient use of aptitudes should improve social conditions on a scientific basis, excluding the influence of familial and social backgrounds. The selection of elites by rational means was a issue of social justice. This conception was closely linked to the project of the comprehensive school promoted by the Compagnons de l'université nouvelle (Companions of the New University), who led the public debate during the 1920-30s. They defended methods of selection including traditional examinations and psychometric tests.

In 1922, Laugier, Piéron and his wife launched the first study on examinations focused on the Certificat d'Études (first diploma at the end of primary school). Then systematic studies were conducted at the Institut national de l'orientation professionnelle or INOP (National Institute of Professional Guidance) and they were enhanced by a large international survey on examinations (1931) supervised by the Carnegie Foundation and the University of Columbia. Another French survey was launched and published in 1934 by a commission headed by Toulouse. Its aims were to fix methods of selection related to the French project of comprehensive schooling. Researchers had collected data on pupils' hereditary features, their personal backgrounds, and their behaviour at school and within their family, and a series of exams had been administered. Toulouse, Laugier and Weinberg favoured the development of these examinations to build a bio-typological and individual booklet as a real biological identity card to care for children during their schooling (Huteau, 2002, p. 139). From 1936, under the supervision of Dr Heuyer, empirical work was carried out by INOP to detect mentally unfit children. Psychologists such as Henri Piéron, the head of the institute, but also physicians and the Minister of Health, Henri Sellier, were at the origin of the survey (Chapoulie, 2006). The Minister created a 'Commission for the Deficient Childhood Facing Moral Danger' and placed it under the presidency of Henri Wallon, the leader of the Compagnons de l'université nouvelle. This commission, which had to carry out the census of mentally unfit children in France, did not last after the fall of the ministry. However, in 1941, the project was taken over by the Vichy government and Alexis Carrel's eugenicist foundation. In 1944, the new commission launched a large-scale survey to study mentally unfit children and to determine the value of human capital in schooling (Institut national d'études démographiques, 1950).

In parallel, during the 1930s, the Statistique générale de France, under the headship of Jean Dessirier and Alfred Sauvy, included studies of economy in its population census (Pollak, 1976). The creation of the Institut de recherches économiques et sociales by Charles Rist had reinforced the importance of economics. This inclusion of demographic and economic issues in State institutions was accelerated under the Vichy regime, when data served the economy of war, particularly the system of rationing and controlling raw materials. The development of statistics entailed a transfer of data management to ministerial organisations. The main providers of statistical data were created by the Vichy government: the National Institute of Hygiene (which become INSERM, or National Institute of Health and Medical Research, after the War), the Alexis Carrel foundation (which become the Institut national d'études démographiques, or National Institute of Demographic Studies), while after the War the Statistique générale de France became INSEE (National Institute of Statistics and Economics). The Commissariat au Plan (Planning Committee), created by Jean Monnet in 1946, recruited economists who had worked with Alfred Sauvy before the War in the Institut de la conjoncture (Economic Research Institute). The creation of the Commissariat au Plan was directly inspired by the Council of Economic Advisers of the US presidency and the Policy Planning Staff of the US State Department (Spenlehauer, 1999).

Demography and the Genesis of a French
Arithmetic of Inequalities in Education

After the War, the measurement of inequalities in education was resumed by the Institut national d'orientation professionnelle (INOP) and the Institut national d'études démographiques (INED). The development of the quantitative French sociology of education can be explained by the development of statistical data in these two institutions. From their eugenics background, INOP and INED developed a modern approach to statistics related to the physiological, mental and social state of the population (Thévenot, 1990). Research on mentally unfit children was continued during the 1950s and supported by new large-scale surveys on the mechanisms of guidance and school selection with a particular focus on gifted pupils (Ravon, 2000). Alain Girard, the leader of these studies within INED (and his British counterpart, David Glass), wanted to sort the elites from the mass of pupils by establishing features, laws and effects of social achievement. In his book *La Réussite sociale en France* (Social Achievement in France) (1961), Girard questioned the intellectual value or aptitudes of individuals fixed at birth and the respective effects of environment, social groups, race and family. Eager to find laws of heredity, quoting research findings on genetics of populations and experimental psychology, Girard considered that the population was divided into unfit and gifted individuals. He thought that the former was a burden on society while the latter, because of the lack of an adjusted use of their gifts, was a source of waste. Like Galton, he was worried by the effect of differential fecundity on the degradation of intellectual capital and the risk of a decline in intellectual levels due to the increase in the number of children in working-class families.

During the 1960s, INOP (which changed its name to INETOP) continued its studies with INED on the intellectual level of pupils in schooling. Granting a request from the Commissariat au Plan, a survey on guidance was launched in 1964 from a sample of 10,000 pupils attending the last grade of lower secondary education (Reuchlin & Bacher, 1967). The planning committee 'Economics and Development' wanted to work on social and pedagogical factors in school guidance in relation to a larger problem concerning education investment and the evolution of active populations (Masson, 2006). A large amount of data on pupils' characteristics were collected by INOP and, later, from additional Centre National de la Recherche Scientifique (National Centre of Scientific Research) allocated funds. The phenomenon was studied over a long period. Viviane Isambert-Jamati, one of the main founders of sociology of education in France, had joined the project. The survey was studying the distribution of IQ tests related to the selection of pupils and drop-outs. Researchers concluded that the democratisation of education required an evaluation of the 'stock of aptitudes' and that inequality of opportunities could be possibly linked to the unequal distribution of intellectual potentialities. They resumed Lancelot Hogben's assumptions and demonstrated that the intellectual level measured by IQ tests had more influence on schooling than the attainment of the baccalaureate. Their conclusions were that, according to equal aptitudes at school measured by IQ, equality led to reduced opportunity for middle-class and working-class pupils.

At the same time, Pierre Bourdieu had developed close links with two administrators of INSEE: Alain Darbel and Claude Seibel (Chapoulie, 2006). They were convinced that statisticians and sociologists had to work together to conceptualise quantitative methods more relevant than those promoted by Paul Lazarfeld in the USA. Bourdieu had great hopes of bringing together the two worlds: social sciences informed by philosophical debates and techniques of engineering worked out within bureaus of statistics. The three friends were contacted by Claude Gruson, the head of INSEE, to join a research project related to the measurement of economic planning and its impact on social progress and equality of opportunities. In 1964, they organised a conference in Arras titled 'The Transformations of the French Society Since the Second World War'. The conference gathered together sociologists, statisticians and economists and the proceedings were published in a collective book titled *Le Partage des bénéfices* (The Share of the Profits) (D'Arras, 1966). In this book, Bourdieu criticised the measurement of 'human stock' and the theory of 'waste of talents' because he considered the main issue was to know how talents or gifts were equally or unequally distributed among social classes. His criticism was also directed against IQ tests and the measurement of school effectiveness, which provided for him a narrow vision of the education system.

However the notion of intellectual capital, conceptualised by Alain Girard as a hereditary transmission, was resumed by Bourdieu and his colleague Jean-Claude Passeron but transformed into a criticism of social conservatism and the ideology of the gift, which legitimated social inequalities in schools. Passeron had met Paul Clerc at INED between 1962 and 1963, while Bourdieu was in contact with the INSEE statisticians. This notion of 'cultural capital' seemed relevant for the two sociologists to distinguish the purely sociological explanation of social reproduction from explanations related to the heredity of genetic backgrounds. In fact, Passeron had discovered that the INED researchers' assumptions which were based on the findings of the 1944 survey and tried to explain 'differential mortality' of children in schooling from different social backgrounds, were relatively vague from the perspective of their genetic, economic or sociological variables. However, with Bourdieu, Passeron was pleased with the use of the notion of 'cultural heritage' by Sauvy and Girard in their paper for the journal *Population* (1965).

Later, Bourdieu and Passeron pursued their criticism against eugenics in their books *Les Héritiers* (1964) and *La Reproduction* (1970). In the first one, they rejected ideas of sorting and organising the education system into a hierarchy according to merit. The measurement of inequalities could not be reduced to some equivalence between socially conditioned aptitudes and rankings based on the measurement of school achievement. This criticism against tests was resumed in the second book. In attacking the statistical analysis of tests, which, for them, served the hidden function of exams, the two sociologists called for a systematic study on the mechanisms of elimination to produce evidence of the link between the functioning of the education system and the maintenance of class relationships. They argued that the trust in tests, beyond assumptions of hereditary characters, served a class endogamy for 'gifted people' and dissimulated a social function of legitimisation of class differences under a technical function of production of qualifications.

The institutional environment was favourable for the two sociologists. From 1971, INSEE developed social statistics: a group of 'social statisticians' included economists, statisticians and sociologists following the Arras conference. Alain Darbel and Claude Seibel published the first social data inspired by their discussions on 'the share of profits' (Œuvrard & Seibel, 2005). Alain Darbel and other statisticians close to Bourdieu's research unit disseminated a new methodology of statistics and social classification at INSEE (Desrosières & Thévenot, 1988). The appointment of Alain Darbel to the Ministry of Education between 1969 and 1971 started the implementation of large-scale surveys inspired by the INED experience while school data on equality of opportunities were developed. Then Claude Seibel was appointed to create and develop the first unit of statistics within the Ministry of Education. Through the creation of frameworks, indicators and data banks, he developed the monitoring and evaluation of the French education system. These data were largely used by sociologists of education to investigate new fields of research into the issue of inequalities.

Conclusion

During the 1920s-30s, the eugenic metrology in the UK was the recipient for methodological innovations in the quantification of social facts. Despite biased philosophical and moral assumptions, these statistics were used to diagnostic vital risks in education and health and to locate social misfits and talents according to a certain vision of social selection. These new sciences (psychology, social biology and economics) were not only producing knowledge about the population, but they also provided tools for the intervention of the Welfare State and served other progressive interests. After 1945, British sociology did not maintain this tradition of political arithmetic established at the London School of Economics. Despite a legacy of empirical and social surveys, the research of Lancelot Hogben and David Glass did not have many followers except Albert H. Hasley and John Goldthorpe, who developed empirical studies on stratification and social mobility. For example, Oxford and Cambridge were slow in taking up social and empiric research and the majority of surveys were designed outside the academic world. During the Sixties, some voices stood up against these positivist approaches and for the promotion of ethnography.

In France, some statistical methods and tools have been borrowed from Anglo-American countries, particularly the theoretical and methodological framework of psychometrics and biometrics. The model of the US large-scale survey took over after the Second World War and it changed the orientation of French social sciences. The institutionalisation of providers of statistical data was inspired by some US and UK examples. Some convergence can be observed between the UK political arithmetic and the issue of inequalities and demography in France. However, some important differences remain. The methods of measurement, their design and application, have been less systematic in France. The lack of stable funding and the difficult emergence of an institution like LSE delayed the development of statistics. France has been more concerned with social hygiene and family while the UK focused the public debate on degeneracy, race and efficiency from the perspective of stronger eugenicist claims. Testing has also not occupied the same place in the French education system.

Without neglecting these national trajectories, this chapter has shown that policy borrowing was active as circulation and translation of knowledge, concepts and tools between the two countries. Similarities appear in the fabrication of measurement of inequalities. This chapter is an attempt to get out from the methodological nationalism in which some researchers could be trapped, according to narratives on the birth and development of sociology of education in each country. This story has to be situated in a larger scientific and political context in order to open the black box in which imaginaries and discourses of truth have been progressively embedded to describe the development of this academic discipline (Furlong & Lawn, 2011). In sociology, as in other disciplines, science and politics can be sometimes strongly interlinked.

References

Blacker, C.P. (1926) *Birth Control and the State: a plea and a forecast.* London: Kegan Paul.

Blacker, C.P. & Glass, D.V. (1937) *The Future of our Population?* London: Population Investigation Committee.

Bourdieu, P. & Passeron, J.-C. (1964) *Les héritiers. Les étudiants et la culture.* Paris: Minuit.

Bourdieu, P. & Passeron, J.-C. (1970) *La reproduction. Éléments pour une théorie du système d'enseignement.* Paris: Minuit.

Bowley, A.L. (1915) *The Nature and Purpose of the Measurement of Social Phenomena.* London: P.S. King & Son.

Bulmer, M. (1985) The Development of Sociology and Empirical Social Research in Britain, in M. Bulmer (Ed.) *Essays on the History of British Sociological Research*, pp. 3-36. Cambridge: Cambridge University Press.

Bulletin de l'alliance nationale pour l'accroissement de la population française (1902) 14, 15 avril, *The Moral and Sociological Causes of Depopulation*, pp. 317-331.

Calder, A. (1985) Mass-Observation 1937-1949, in M. Bulmer (Ed.) *Essays on the History of British Sociological Research*, pp. 121-136. Cambridge: Cambridge University Press.

Carr-Saunders, A. (1922) *The Population Problems*. Oxford: Clarendon Press.

Carrel, A. (1935) *L'homme, cet inconnu*. Paris: Plon.

Chapoulie, J.-M. (2005) *Sociologues et sociologies. La France des années 1960*. Paris: L'Harmattan.

Chapoulie, J.-M. (2006) Les nouveaux spécialistes des sciences sociales comme 'experts' de la politique scolaire en France 1945-1962, *Genèses*, 3(64), 124-145.

Dahrendorf, R. (1995) *A History of the London School of Economics and Political Science 1895-1995*. Oxford: Oxford University Press.

D'Arras (1966) *Le partage des bénéfices, Expansion et inégalité en France*. Paris: Minuit.

Desrosières, A. (1993) *La politique des grands nombres. Histoire de la raison statistique*. Paris: La Découverte.

Desrosières, A. & Thévenot, L. (1988) *Les catégories socioprofessionnelles*. Paris: La Découverte.

Floud, J.E., Halsey, A.H. & Martin, F.M. (1956) *Social Class and Educational Opportunity*. London: William Heinemann.

Foucault, M. (2004) *Sécurité, territoire, population, cours au Collège de France 1977-78*. Paris: Gallimard-Seuil.

Furlong, J. & Lawn, M. (2011) *Disciplines of Education. Their Role in the Future of Education Research*. London: Routledge.

Gessain, D. & Vincent, P. (1945) Quelques aspects quantitatifs et qualitatifs de la population française, *Cahiers de la Fondation Française pour l'étude des problèmes humains*, March, 19-32.

Girard, A. (1961) La réussite sociale en France, *INED*, Cahier no. 38.

Glass, D.L. (Ed.) (1954) *Social Mobility in Britain*. London: Routledge & Kegan Paul.

Gray, J.L. (1936) *The Nation's Intelligence*. London: Watts & Co.

Halbwachs, M. & Sauvy, A. (1936) *Le point de vue du nombre*. Édition critique sous la direction de Marie Jaisson et Éric Brian, Paris, Institut national d'études démographiques, 2005.

Halsey, A.H., Floud, J.E. & Anderson, C.A. (Eds) (1961) *Education, Economy and Society*. New York: The Free Press of Glencoe.

Hogben, L. (Ed.) (1938) *Political Arithmetic. A Symposium of Population Studies*. New York: The Macmillan Company.

Huteau, M. (2002) *Psychologie, psychiatrie et société sous la troisième République. La biocratie d'Édouard Toulouse (1865-1947)*. Paris: L'Harmattan.

Institut national d'études démographiques (1950) *Le Niveau intellectuel des enfants d'âge scolaire*. Paris: Presses universitaires de France.

Kent, R. (1985) The Emergence of the Sociological Survey, 1887-1939, in M. Bulmer (Ed.) *Essays on the History of British Sociological Research*, pp. 52-69. Cambridge: Cambridge University Press.

Masson, P. (2006) Le financement de la sociologie française: les conventions de recherche de la DGRST dans les années soixante, *Genèses*, 1(62), 110-128.

Mazon, B. (1988) *Aux origines de l'EHESS. Le rôle du mécénat américain*. Paris: Éd. du Cerf.

Normand, R. (2011) *Gouverner la réussite scolaire. Une arithmétique politique des inégalités*. Bern: Peter Lang, Presses de l'École Normale Supérieure.

Œuvrard, F. & Seibel, C. (2005) Le développement des études sociales dans le système statistique public, in J.-M. Chapoulie, *Sociologues et sociologies. La France des années 1960*, pp. 87-98. Paris: L'Harmattan.

Pinell, P. (1977) L'école obligatoire et les recherches en pédagogie au début du XXe siècle, *Cahiers internationaux de sociologie*, 63, 341-362.

Pollak, M. (1976) La planification des sciences sociales, *Actes de la recherche en sciences sociales*, 2(2-3), La production de l'idéologie dominante, 105-121.

Ravon, B. (2000) *L'« échec scolaire ». Histoire d'un problème public*. Paris: In Press Éditions.

Reuchlin, M. & Bacher, F. (1967) Enquête sur l'orientation à la fin du premier cycle secondaire, *BINOP*, 23(5), 321-329.

Rosental, P.A. (2003) *L'Intelligence démographique. Sciences et politiques des populations en France (1930-1960)*. Paris: Odile Jacob.

Sauvy, A. & Girard, A. (1965) Les diverses classes sociales devant l'enseignement. Mise au point générale des résultats, *Population*, 2, 205-232.

Schneider, W.H. (1990) *Quality and Quantity: the quest for biological regeneration in twentieth century France*. Cambridge: Cambridge University Press.

Scot, M. (2005) *La London School of Economics and Political Science et le Welfare State. Science et politique en Grande-Bretagne, 1940-1979*. Paris: L'Harmattan.

Soloway, R.A. (1990) *Demography and Degeneration: eugenics and the declining birthrate in twentieth-century Britain*. Chapel Hill: University of North Carolina Press.

Spenlehauer, V. (1999) Intelligence gouvernementale et sciences sociales, *Politix*, 12(48), 95-128.

Sutherland, G. (1984) *Ability, Merit, and Measurement: mental testing and English education, 1880-1940*. Oxford: Oxford University Press.

Sutter, J. (1950) *L'Eugénique: problèmes, méthodes, résultants*. Paris: Presses universitaires de France.

Tawney, R.H. (1922) *Secondary Education for All. A Policy for Labour*. London: The Labour Party.

Tawney, R.H. (1931) *Equality*. London: Unwin Books.

Thévenot, L. (1990) La Politique des statistiques: les origines sociales des enquêtes de mobilité sociale, *Annales ESC*, no. 6, November-December.

Whitehead, F. (1985) The Government Social Survey, in M. Bulmer (Ed.) *Essays on the History of British Sociological Research*, pp. 83-100. Cambridge: Cambridge University Press.

Wooldridge, A. (1994) *Measuring the Mind. Education and Psychology in England. 1860-1990.* Cambridge: Cambridge University Press.

Notes on Contributors

Marcelo Caruso holds a degree in Educational Studies from the University of Buenos Aires, a PhD from the University of Munich and a habilitation from Humboldt University in Berlin. He is the Chair of History of Education at Humboldt University. He is one of the editors-in-chief of the German Yearbook for History of Education and a member of the editorial boards of *Paedagogica Historica* and the German *Zeitschrift für Pädagogik*.

Inés Dussel is Professor and Researcher at the Department of Educational Research (DIE/CINVESTAV) in Mexico. She received her PhD at the University of Wisconsin-Madison. She was a Senior Researcher at FLACSO/Argentina before moving to Mexico. She has worked on the history and theory of curriculum and pedagogy, and is currently doing research on the introduction of digital media in schools.

Joyce Goodman is Professor of History of Education, Pro-Vice-Chancellor and Dean of the Faculty of Education, Health and Social Care at the University of Winchester. She is former editor of *History of Education*, past president of the History of Education Society and former secretary of the International Standing Conference for the History of Education. She has published widely on women and education. Her most recent books include *Women and Education: major themes in education* (Routledge, 2011, 4 volumes) with Jane Martin, and *Girls' Secondary Education in the Western World* (Palgrave, 2010) with James Albisetti and Rebecca Rogers. Her current research focuses on empire and internationalism in girls' schooling and the work of women in and for education.

Ian Grosvenor is Professor of Urban Educational History and Deputy Pro-Vice-Chancellor for Cultural Engagement at the University of Birmingham, United Kingdom.

Joakim Landahl is a researcher at the Department of Education, Stockholm University. His research concentrates on the history of school discipline, childhood, the teaching profession, and relations between pupils and teachers. Currently he is working on the history of interaction rituals in classrooms.

Martin Lawn is a Professorial Research Fellow at the Centre for Educational Sociology, University of Edinburgh. He is the editor of the *European Educational Research Journal,* academic journal of the European Educational Research Association. Recent books include: *An Atlantic Crossing? The Work of the International Examinations Inquiry, its Researchers, Methods and Influence* (Symposium Books, Comparative Histories of Education Series, 2008) and *Modelling the Future: exhibitions and the materiality of education* (Symposium Books, Comparative Histories of Education Series, 2009).

Christian Lundahl is Professor in Education at Karlstad University and Associate Professor at the Department of Education, Stockholm University. He specialises in the history of assessments, evaluation and Swedish educational research.

Romuald Normand is Associate Professor of Sociology of Education at the École Normale Supérieure, Lyon, France. He works on comparative education policies and politics, Europeanisation and lifelong learning, higher education and research, transformation of the state and New Public Management. He is a convenor of the Network 28 'Sociologies of European Education' at the European Educational Research Association and member of the editorial board of the *British Journal of Sociology of Education.*

Siân Roberts is Head of Collections Development at Birmingham Archives and Heritage and Honorary Research Fellow at the School of Education, University of Birmingham, United Kingdom.

Noah W. Sobe is Associate Professor of Cultural and Educational Policy Studies at Loyola University Chicago, where he specialises in the history of education and in comparative international education. He researches globalisation and accountability practices in education in both their present and historical forms. He is the author of *Provincializing the Worldly Citizen: Yugoslav student and teacher travel in the inter-war era* and editor of *American Post-Conflict Education Reform: from the Spanish-American War to Iraq.* He is the co-editor of the journal *European Education.*